ALL CHANGE!

**Visiting the Byways of Britain's
Railway Network**

Published by AA Publishing, a trading name of AA Media Limited, whose registered office is Fanum House, Basing View, Basingstoke, Hampshire RG21 4EA. Registered number 06112600

Packaged for AA Media Limited by OutHouse!, Shalbourne, Marlborough SN8 3QJ

For OutHouse!:
Managing editor Sue Gordon
Art editors Dawn Terrey and Heather McCarry
Picture researcher Julian Holland

For AA Publishing:
Production Lyn Kirby

First published in the UK in 2009
Reprinted May and November 2009

A04333

ISBN: 978-0-7495-6605-0

Repro and colour separation by Imaging MM, London
Printed in China by C&C Offset Printing Co., Ltd

This edition printed for PR Books

▽ As goods traffic began to decline in the 1950s, British Railways increasingly sold off redundant rolling stock, especially box vans, whose bodies could easily be adapted for other purposes. Often these were used on farms for storage or animal accommodation, and many remain scattered over the landscape. Most are derelict, but this one is still earning its keep as a shepherd's hut, high in the Pennines and miles from the nearest railway.

ALL CHANGE!

Visiting the Byways of Britain's Railway Network

Paul Atterbury

AA

CONTENTS

◁ In the late 1940s a veteran Johnson 0-4-4 tank locomotive rests in the sun at Tewkesbury.

▷ An old GWR Class 5700 tank locomotive takes water at Bilson
Junction, in the Forest of Dean, in 1965.

INTRODUCTION

'All Change!', the well-known phrase indicating the end of a train journey or the change from a major to a minor line, is also reflective of the massive changes to the railway network over the last 50 years.

Many people remember the richness of the railway experience that was once a part of everyday life in Britain. Grand stations, main lines, high-speed trains and busy commuter services were, and to some extent still are, the obvious face of the railway. However, what all this has tended to obscure is the turmoil of activity going on behind the smooth façade – those often overlooked aspects of railway life that made up the complete picture.

This book explores these byways of the railways, past and present. With a mix of hitherto unseen or unfamiliar photographs, postcards and ephemera, it visits branch lines long closed, branch lines that against the odds are alive, freight and industrial lines, docks and harbours, lines dedicated to coal and mineral traffic, narrow gauge and miniature railways, and lines serving military establishments and hospitals. Railways have always played a part in childhood, often generating lifelong enthusiasms, so the book also covers toy trains and model railways, even children's books and trainspotting. With its emphasis on forgotten parts of railway history, this book celebrates the multi-layered diversity that is the true story of Britain's railway network.

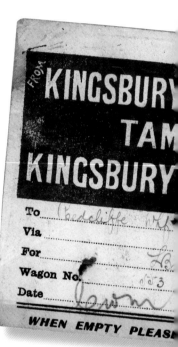

△ Postcards offer an interesting insight into the history of the railways. Many were issued to celebrate what seem to us minor events and insignificant places. This card is from a series published to celebrate the construction and opening in 1904, by King Edward VII and Queen Alexandra, of the Elan valley reservoir scheme in mid-Wales, built to supply fresh water to Birmingham. The royal couple travelled there on a railway specially built to access the remote site.

▷ Model railways and toy trains have been integral to children's lives for well over a century, and Hornby has always been one of the best-known names. Frank Hornby launched his 0 gauge tinplate railway system in the 1920s with a range of locomotives, rolling stock and accessories that continued to expand until the early 1960s. This is a 1930s No. 2 clockwork tank locomotive in Southern Railway colours, complete with its characteristic red box.

◁ There were many obscure corners of the national railway map. Typical was the East Kent Railway, built to serve the Kent coalfields from the early 20th century. Much of this once-extensive network had disappeared by the early 1950s, leaving only a short section to connect the mine at Tilmanstone to the main line. This survived until the Kentish pits were closed in the 1980s. This 1957 photograph shows an East Kent train emerging from Golgotha tunnel, en route from Tilmanstone to Shepherdswell.

△ There used to be branch lines all over Britain, but few survived the closures of the 1960s and 1970s. A rare example still in use is the line from Norwich to Sheringham via Cromer, now the only branch line in Norfolk in the national network. This photograph shows a modern train departing from the station at Sheringham, clearly the end of the line.

△ The railways were prodigious producers of paperwork, and plenty survives today to tell the story both of railways long forgotten and the way of life they represented. Readily accessible in large quantities are tickets, promotional leaflets, baggage and carriage labels, wagon labels, operational instructions – and much else besides. A typical example is this Midland Railway wagon label, perhaps from the Edwardian era, a survivor that brings to life the lost worlds of railways and coal mining.

△ There was a time when everything travelled by train, and until the 1970s goods trains were a common sight all over the British network. With their apparently random mix of wagons, they hinted at a secret railway world of which ordinary passengers knew very little. In the early 1960s, when this photograph was taken, this world was already in decline but the appeal of the goods train remained universal. On the derelict platforms of Baguley station, in Cheshire, young boys watch the slow passage of a mixed goods, headed by an 8F Class locomotive.

THE WEST COUNTRY

THE GUNNISLAKE BRANCH

ONE OF THE MORE EXTRAORDINARY survivals of the 1960s closures is the branch line to Gunnislake from Plymouth. Today this is a delightfully rural route, climbing into a remote Cornish landscape and giving little hint of its complicated history. It started life as the Tamar, Kit Hill & Callington Railway in the early 1860s, a quarry line that got nowhere until it was reformed as the Callington & Calstock Railway in 1869. This in turn became the East Cornwall Mineral Railway, and the route finally opened in 1872 with an inclined plane linking it to quarries on the river Tamar. In 1908 the last piece was put in place, a line to Bere Alston, where it met the LSWR's main line to Plymouth.

◁ After leaving Plymouth, the former LSWR main line, now the Gunnislake branch, runs along beside the river Tamar. In 1981 a DMU makes its way north from St Budeaux towards Bere Alston.

▷ Calstock station, seen here in about 1914, is at the western end of the Tamar viaduct. Originally, a long inclined plane connected the railway to the quays below, but this was replaced by a wagon hoist, whose operating machinery stands above the viaduct.

▽ The Bere Alston & Calstock Railway had to build only 4 miles of track to its mainline connection, but the Tamar was in the middle, necessitating the building of a great viaduct. This photograph shows it under construction in about 1907, while passengers on a crowded steamer inspect it.

▽ Elegant, impressive and with 12 arches reaching a height of 120ft above the Tamar, Calstock viaduct is the highlight of the journey. It is the country's largest viaduct to have been built from concrete blocks, cast on site and finished to resemble stone. This is a 1990s view.

London and South Western Ry. 797

WATERLOO TO

CALSTOCK

Stoke Climsland Station

△ The penultimate station before the end of the line at Callington was Stoke Climsland, later renamed Luckett. This Edwardian view shows the basic nature of the buildings on the line, then operated by the Plymouth, Devonport & South Western Junction Railway.

London and South Western Ry. 787
—
WATERLOO TO
STOKE CLIMSLAND

Gunnislake Station. 16040

◁ Gunnislake is now the terminus of the branch, the line to Callington having been closed in 1966. In the early 1900s, as seen here, freight traffic was the railway's lifeline.

▷ Today the original buildings at the Gunnislake terminus have gone, replaced by an even more rudimentary bus shelter. This 1990s view shows quite a busy summer scene.

▷ In 1958 Class 02 tank locomotive No. 30225 runs round its train at Callington, prior to hauling it back to Plymouth. The little signal cabin is also visible in the postcard below right.

▽ Dating from 1962, this timetable brochure shows how British Railways worked hard to develop tourist traffic on routes around Plymouth.

RAIL·ROAD RIVER·SEA

EXCURSIONS
TOURS
TIMETABLES

PLYMOUTH
and selected stations
in SOUTH DEVON and CORNWALL
WESTERN REGION

18th JUNE to
9th SEPTEMBER
INCLUSIVE, 1962
PADDINGTON STATION, W.2

▷ When this postcard was sent in 1909 from Callington to Montana, in the United States, the station was sometimes known as Callington Road.

THE SEVERN BEACH BRANCH

TODAY SEVERN BEACH station lies at the end of a popular branch line from Bristol, the surviving section of a once-complex local network. In 1865 the Bristol, Port, Railway & Pier Company opened a line along the Avon from Hotwells to Avonmouth, where the eponymous pier was situated. Initially isolated, the line was soon linked to existing railways. A heavily engineered 4-mile extension connected it via Clifton to the Bristol-to-Birmingham main line, and to the north another extension via Severn Beach joined it to the Bristol & South Wales Union's route near what is now the entrance to the Severn Tunnel. The sections to Hotwells and beyond Severn Beach were closed in the 20th century.

▽ The short section of the branch from Bristol to Sea Mills via Montpelier and Clifton is dramatic, with steep cuttings, viaducts and a long tunnel. Here, in July 1979, an afternoon service to Severn Beach has just left Clifton Down station, and the single-car DMU is about to enter the tunnel.

G.W.R.

Clifton Down

◁ There used to be plenty of freight traffic on the Severn Beach line, thanks to its many links to other lines serving local industry and the docks. The freight link to Avonmouth nowadays is via the Henbury loop. In 1959, this former GWR Hall Class locomotive, No. 5914 'Ripon Hall', banks a long train of box wagons running towards Avonmouth on the Severn Beach line. The train has come from the South Wales line, via Pilning.

REVISED

PASSENGER TRAIN SERVICES

ON WEEKDAYS

COMMENCING

MONDAY, 23rd NOVEMBER, 1964

BETWEEN	BRISTOL (Temple Meads)
	CLIFTON DOWN
	AVONMOUTH DOCK
	SEVERN BEACH

FOR DETAILS SEE OTHER SIDE

British Railways
Western Region

▷ This card, posted in 1905 as a birthday greeting, shows the long-established popularity of Clifton as a place for outings and recreation. Railway access from the centre of Bristol had greatly increased its appeal from the 1880s.

Promenade and Fountain, Clifton Down

▽ Despite its industrial associations, the Severn Beach line has been listed among Britain's most scenic railway routes. Certainly there are spectacular views, notably out across the Severn estuary with the M4 motorway bridge in the background. This photograph was taken at the point where the Severn Way footpath crosses the line.

△ Industrial scenes can make the journey exciting. Looking like something from America's Midwest, this is a coal-handling plant near Avonmouth. Also of interest on this part of the route are the Merry Go Round coal trains still in regular use.

▽ The vast and largely abandoned platforms at Avonmouth station dwarf the modern DMU trains that operate the route. They are also a reminder of past glories, a theme not uncommon on the Severn Beach branch today.

▷ A battered old Derby DMU, bearing Welsh Valley Lines badging, rests at Severn Beach while the driver poses in the cab. These popular and long-familiar vehicles were the last to offer passengers seated in the front of the carriage the driver's view of the journey and the track ahead.

▽ Severn Beach, where there is another long and largely disused platform, is very clearly the end of the line, although trains used to continue north from here towards Pilning. Here, in April 1982, the few passengers (mostly women) travelling to Severn Beach on an afternoon DMU service from Bristol Temple Meads stroll away from the train.

THE MORETONHAMPSTEAD BRANCH

DESPITE THE CHALLENGING NATURE of its hilly landscape, South Devon was remarkably well served by branch lines. An early example was the Moretonhampstead & South Devon Railway, a broad gauge line running north from Newton Abbot along the Bovey valley. Opened in 1866, it was soon absorbed by the South Devon Railway and then by the GWR. Its connections included the old Haytor Tramway, dating back to 1820, and a rural route to Exeter via Heathfield, Chudleigh and Christow, which was completed in 1903. The scenic and steeply graded line was important for mineral traffic, notably clay, and this kept a section south from Heathfield open long past the end of passenger services in 1959.

▷ By the 1950s passenger traffic was much diminished. Here, in the summer of 1958, a few months before closure, a GWR 2-6-2 tank locomotive hauls its single carriage towards Newton Abbot, near Teigngrace Halt. The wide trackbed is a reminder of the line's broad gauge origins.

▽ North of Bovey the route is often hidden in woods beside the fast-flowing Bovey river. Handsome granite bridges reveal the railway's early date, and there are are other occasional survivals, including this trackside concrete hut.

◁ At Heathfield there was a junction with the rural route to Exeter via Chudleigh, which goes straight on. This picture was taken at a quiet moment, perhaps in the 1920s. There is little passenger activity, but it was in any case the potteries, whose chimneys are seen to the left, that always generated most of the line's traffic.

▷ North from Newton Abbot the line followed closely the old Stover canal, traces of which can be seen. This section, north to Heathfield, remained in use long after closure in 1959, and today the track is still in place, giving a misleading sense of life and activity.

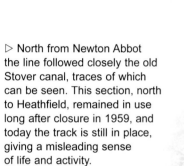

△ In 1988 there was regular clay traffic between Heathfield and St Blazey, in Cornwall. In July of that year, Class 50 locomotive 'Defiance' (since preserved) waits with its two clay wagons while the Teign bridge crossing gates are closed behind it.

▽ At Bovey Tracey the track has disappeared beneath a road, but the main 1866 station building survives, now used as a museum and heritage centre. The grassy verge represents the platform (seen in the postcard to the right), but access is now only from the other side.

▷ This Edwardian card shows Bovey station in its original setting, with passengers awaiting the arrival of the train for Moretonhampstead.

G. W. Railway Station.

Chapman & Son, Dawlish

G.W.R.

BOVEY

△ In the 1930s Lustleigh was a delightful station, built in the railway's typical granite style and noted for its gardens. Today the building survives as a private house.

The Station Lustleigh

▷ In April 1957, 5101 Class tank locomotive No. 5183 sits in Moretonhampstead platform while the driver has a word with the guard and a rather well-dressed man waits to board. Perhaps it is his friend who is taking the photograph.

◁ The terminus station at Moretonhampstead was set well below the town, necessitating the bus connection that features in this Edwardian view. Also to be seen here is the covered train shed. Today the site is an industrial estate, but the engine shed survives.

▽ This 1907 card shows the character of this Devon hill town. From 1929, when the GWR took over the famous Manor House and converted it into a luxury hotel, the station gained a new lease of life.

G. W. R.

MORETON-HAMPSTEAD

▽ For the final approach to Moretonhampstead, the line left the hills and the steep river valley, crossing open fields on a low embankment, still clearly visible today.

Green Hill.

Moreton Hampstead. B 3160

THE PORTLAND BRANCH

PORTLAND'S LONG HISTORY as the source of the stone that bears its name ensured that railways came early to the island. Local quarry lines were commonplace, but the first definable line was the Portland, or Merchants, Railway, linking quarries on the western heights to Castletown pier. Opened in 1826 and horse-operated with inclines, it survived until 1939. Traces of it remain, including bridges. Next, from about 1849, came the broad gauge Admiralty line for building the harbour piers and the dockyard. Much more important was the Weymouth & Portland Railway's link to the mainland across Chesil Beach, opened in 1865. Initially mixed gauge, this was operated jointly from the start by the GWR and the L&SWR. In 1902 an extension to Easton completed the line, and this then remained in use until 1965. Today much of the route survives, and sections of it can be walked.

▷ The original route of the Weymouth & Portland Railway was from Melcombe Regis, north of Weymouth, to Portland, and it always operated independently. There were several intermediate stations, of which the most important was Rodwell, set in a cutting south of Weymouth. Here, on a lazy summer's day in the Edwardian era, the train, and its crew, wait for the photographer.

522   CHESIL BEACH AND PORTLAND HARBOUR.

◁ This 1960s card, one of the most popular views of Portland, shows the route of the railway across Chesil Beach towards Weymouth, visible in the distance beyond the harbour.

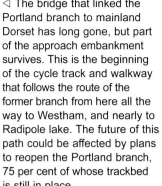

◁ The bridge that linked the Portland branch to mainland Dorset has long gone, but part of the approach embankment survives. This is the beginning of the cycle track and walkway that follows the route of the former branch from here all the way to Westham, and nearly to Radipole lake. The future of this path could be affected by plans to reopen the Portland branch, 75 per cent of whose trackbed is still in place.

△ Stone traffic had brought the railways of Portland into being and that traffic, along with supplies for the Admiralty dockyard, remained important right up to closure in 1965. Here, at the very end of the railway's life, a long line of open wagons loaded with the distinctive white stone is hauled towards the mainland.

▷ The branch ended at Easton, in the heart of Portland. Its sizeable station is shown here not long after the line opened. All that remains now is the road bridge and part of the cutting that housed the station.

EASTON & CHURCH HOPE RAILWAY

The Stone Railway, Portland

△ Portland's earliest railways were primitive lines built to serve the quarries. This Edwardian card shows in the distance one of the inclined planes linking the quarries on the heights to the harbour piers.

◁ The best part of the route for exploration is the old trackbed along Portland's remote and rocky eastern shore towards the terminus of the 1902 extension, at Easton. Still to be seen are reminders of the railway's important role in the stone trade, including the abandoned remains of old stone wagons.

SCRAPBOOK : THE WEST COUNTRY

THERE IS MUCH TO ENJOY in the railway history of the West Country. Collected here is a wide range of images from the 1860s to the 1960s that offer an insight into the railway past of Cornwall, Devon, Dorset and Somerset. There are minor lines, branches and stations, some long lost and others that survive but now look very different. There are minor trains on major lines, and scenes of railway life, both passenger and freight, that are reminders of a time when the Southwest was dependent upon its extensive network. Throughout the century covered by these images, the railways were at the heart of commercial and domestic life, and they used their promotional skills to maintain that position.

▽ On a sunny morning in May 1954 a former GWR auto train makes its way slowly across the eastern approach viaduct of Brunel's great Royal Albert bridge, then approaching its centenary. The train is a local from Saltash to Plymouth, the kind of railway service increasingly challenged by bus and car.

▷ During the summer of 1957, 0-6-0 PT tank locomotive No. 8421 hauls its short train away from Truro and into the deep cutting that marks the start of the Falmouth branch. At that time, similar scenes were an everyday experience throughout Britain's massive railway network. The Falmouth branch is still open today, but the vehicles, and the infrastructure, are very different.

◁ The GWR was famous for its publicity material, much of which promoted holiday routes. Typical is the series of bookmarks from the 1930s, in this case featuring Penzance and St Michael's Mount.

◁ A short platform, two lamps, a nameboard and a classic GWR metal pagoda shelter is all there was to Goonhavern Halt, on the remote north Cornwall route between Newquay and Chacewater. A bicycle leaning against the railings is the only evidence of life; maybe the owner is inside the shelter, or does it belong to the photographer? The station, and the line, closed in 1963.

▷ Yards full of wagons loaded with barrels of clay indicate the real business of the branch line to Fowey in this 1920s view. Although carriages line the station platforms, there are very few passengers to be seen. Passenger traffic ended in 1965, but the branch remains busy with clay trains to this day.

▷ Dartmoor stretches into the distance as a train bound for Princetown pulls away from Ingra Tor Halt. This branch line, with some of the best views in southern England, closed completely in 1956. Sections of the trackbed can be walked.

▽ This photograph, which dates from the late 1860s or early 1870s, shows Ivy Bridge station, as it was then called, on the main line east of Plymouth. It is broad gauge days, and the Brunel-designed buildings look new and clean. Beyond it is the viaduct, originally built for Brunel's atmospheric railway scheme. Still visible at this time is the strengthening added after the plan was abandoned in the late 1840s.

◁ The line to Looe from Liskeard has a very long history, stretching back to 1825. It was built for the clay trade, but carried passengers from 1879. The link from Coombe Junction to Liskeard opened in 1901, and the GWR ran it from 1909. This card, showing a smart locomotive and carriages in the station at Looe, dates from about that period.

G.W.R.

Looe

△ Steam survived on the Looe branch until the 1960s, as this photograph indicates. Working hard, a large 2-6-2 tank locomotive hauls its train round the steep horseshoe curve into Liskeard.

◁ This is Coombe station in the 1930s, with a distant view of a freight train crossing the viaduct that carries the main line. Beyond the platform is the old clay line to Moorswater and Caradon, opened in 1844. Passenger trains between Looe and Liskeard still reverse at Coombe Junction.

▷ ▽ One of the more remote of the West Country branches, the line from Upwey to Abbotsbury opened in 1885. Inspired by unfounded rumours of local iron ore deposits, it had to rely on minimal passenger traffic and was eventually abandoned in 1952. The major intermediate station on the branch was Portesham, seen left in the early 1960s, long after closure. The 1937 view of the station, below, is – for this line – quite a busy one, and there is a Camping Coach parked in a siding. The station building is now a private house.

3W

TRAIN SERVICES

From 6 September 1965 to 12 June 1966
(or until further notice)

between
**CASTLE CARY, YEOVIL (PEN MILL)
BRIDPORT, MAIDEN NEWTON
DORCHESTER WEST and WEYMOUTH**
also
**BOURNEMOUTH CENTRAL, POOLE
SWANAGE, WAREHAM, WOOL
DORCHESTER SOUTH and WEYMOUTH**

△ This 1965/66 brochure promotes mainline services between Bournemouth and Weymouth, and branch services to Bridport and Swanage. Both branches subsequently closed.

▷ Until the 1980s railway companies ran much more than just trains. This shows the GWR passenger ferry boat *The Mew* operating the Kingswear-to-Dartmouth service in the summer of 1945.

▽ Another famous Dorset branch line (though its mainline connection, at Axminster, was actually in Devon) served Lyme Regis. Opened as an independent concern in 1903 after a lengthy gestation period, it was soon in difficulties and in 1906 was absorbed by the LSWR. It closed in November 1965, but not before it had made its name among enthusiasts as one of the last habitats of that late Victorian classic, the Adams radial tank locomotive.

△ It is 16 April 1964 and in three weeks' time West Moors station in east Dorset will close, along with the lines to Salisbury and Ringwood. This couple, perhaps father and daughter posing for mother, are probably making the most of it while they can.

△ A couple in summery clothes leave the DMU at Stogumber, on the Minehead branch in north Somerset, in August 1968. In January 1971 the branch closed, but it subsequently reopened as a preserved line.

THE WEST SOMERSET MINERAL RAILWAY

SOME OF BRITAIN'S EARLIEST railways were built to link mineral deposits to ports and harbours. While not especially early, the West Somerset Mineral Railway was certainly one of the more unusual. Authorized in 1855 and fully opened four years later, the railway was built to transport iron ore from the Brendon Hills to Watchet harbour. The ore deposits were high on the hill, necessitating a long inclined plane that connected the upper workings with the railway below. In 1865 a passenger service was introduced from Watchet to Comberow, at the foot of the incline. In the same year it was taken over by the Ebbw Vale Steel, Iron and Coal Company. The mines closed in 1883 but passenger services continued to run until 1898. In 1907 rising ore prices brought about a reopening, but this was short-lived, and by 1910 the railway was abandoned.

▷ This famous image shows the celebrations held on 4 July 1907 to mark the reopening of the West Somerset Mineral Railway. Optimism clearly reigned at this sign of revived local prosperity, and the beflagged locomotive, fresh from its former life with the Metropolitan Railway (part of London's expanding underground network), is ready to haul the first train. In the event, it was to be a false dawn as by 1910 the railway had closed forever.

◁ For a relatively minor and somewhat remote line, the West Somerset Mineral Railway was well photographed, and there are many pictures to tell its rather extraordinary story. Though passenger services were, for much of its life, incidental to the ore traffic, stations and structures were well built and fully staffed, as this photograph indicates.

◁ ▽ The railway's most famous feature was the Brendon Hill inclined plane, opened in September 1859 to link the upper ore workings with the main line far below. It was 1,100 yards long, and the slope was 1 in 4. Cable-powered, it was self-operated for over 20 years, the weight of the loaded descending wagons pulling up the empty ascending ones, but in 1883 a stationary steam engine took over haulage. The incline featured in local postcards. The card on the left shows the reopening ceremony of 4 July 1907. At the bottom of the incline is the ex-Metropolitan locomotive, with its Underground railway condensing equipment still in place. The card below, although issued in the Edwardian era, shows the incline during the 1890s, when passenger services were operating prior to the first closure.

Published by HERBERT H. HOLE, Williton

Brendon Hill (Incline)

◁ This view, looking down the incline, was probably taken when the railway was reopened. Comberow station and the water tower can be seen at the bottom of the hill.

◁ The West Somerset Mineral Railway had its own station at Watchet, where it met the GWR Minehead branch. There were also passenger stations at Roadwater and Comberow. In addition, stations were built on the upper section, above the incline, at Langham Hill and Gupworthy, but it is unlikely that these were ever used by scheduled passenger services.

▷ This image, seemingly from the wilds of North America, actually shows a platelayer at work on the West Somerset Mineral Railway. It is the 1890s, towards the end of the line's life, and the track looks overgrown, but some form of maintenance and inspection process was still being carried out.

◁ The railway was finally abandoned in 1910, and the track was removed in 1917 to aid the war effort. From that point, the line was allowed to disappear back into the landscape. Today much of the route is inaccessible but, as this photograph and those on the opposite page indicate, plenty remains to be seen. They were taken in the 1980s. This one shows a surviving overbridge near the incline.

◁ The stone engine house built for the stationary steam engine that was brought in to operate the incline from 1883 survives as a romantic and overgrown ruin when photographed a century later.

△ Although the track and much of the infrastructure was removed in 1917, some things remained, such as these sleepers, still in place in the 1980s.

△ ▷ The route of the Brendon Hill incline is clearly marked on the landscape, though by the 1980s it was more overgrown and partly hidden by trees, as can be seen in these two photographs. This will be an enduring monument to an obscure but alluring part of the railway history of Southwest England.

STONE & CLAY

THE MAJOR INDUSTRIES of the West Country have long been clay and stone. By the time the railways came, the great days of the copper mines had gone, and tin was also in decline. By contrast, the trade in slate, granite and other stone increased in the 19th century, and the first railways in the West Country were built to connect quarries and mines to local harbours. Even more important was the clay traffic, mostly from the huge deposits north of St Austell, first exploited commercially in the late 18th century.

Cheese Wring Quarry, near Liskeard

△ Most quarries used railways, even if they were not connected to main lines. This Edwardian postcard shows some of the lines in the Cheesewring quarry, near Liskeard. These were part of the Caradon network.

△ An early Cornish railway was the Pentewan, opened in 1829 to connect quarries with a port near St Austell. Initially narrow gauge, it was converted to standard gauge from 1874, but closed in 1918 due to silting in the harbour. Part of it was a sand line, whose remains could still be seen near the harbour in 1992.

△ Sometime in the 1990s a Class 08 shunter hauls clay wagons along the quayside at Fowey.

▽ China clay has been the mainstay of the Fowey branch for decades. Here, in 1989, a Class 37 diesel-hauled train crosses the Golant embankment

G.W.R.
4237
TO
FOWEY

△ One of the best-loved and longest-lasting of the Cornish clay lines ran up through woods from Boscarne Junction, near Bodmin, to Wenford Bridge. In its latter years it was famous as the last home of the Beattie well tank locomotive, one of which is seen here on a typically ungated level crossing.

△ Another clay line was the goods-only Meledor Mill branch, which ran south from the Par-to-Newquay main line, near St Columb Road. Here, in August 1962, a double-headed enthusiasts' brake van special visits the branch, on a tour of Cornish mineral lines.

△ Another long-established clay network lies north of Liskeard, in the Moorswater and Caradon region. Here, in 1988, a Class 37 locomotive hauls a clay train to Coombe, with the mainline viaduct in the background.

▷ A timeless GWR industrial scene as an old 0-6-0 tank locomotive propels its goods train down the short branch from St Blazey to Par harbour in 1954. The low viaduct carries the main line towards St Austell.

WEST COUNTRY PORTS & HARBOUR

THE MAJOR DOCK COMPLEXES in the West Country have always been Plymouth and Bristol, and the scale of these has tended to overshadow the many smaller docks in Somerst, Dorset, Devon and Cornwall. Some were general purpose, serving predominantly local needs while others, for example the Cornish ports, were dedicated to particular cargoes, such as stone or clay. What they nearly all had in common was that they were railway-operated. Many of the smaller docks have closed since the 1960s. Few survivors retain their railway links.

G. W. R.

AVONMOUTH ROYAL EDWARD DOCK

MIDLAND RAILWAY Co. G F 155
9/094 *Aug 15* 189
From AVONMOUTH DOCK
To *West Pennyard*
Company *Bath*
Route *Bath*
Wagon No. *...*
Consignee *H. Cottrell...*

◁ Long famous as a naval dockyard, Plymouth developed in the 19th century into a major commercial port with a series of specialized docks, including Millbay, Turnchapel, Cattewater and Devonport (for the Royal Navy), all rail-connected. Here, in the late 1950s, a shunting crew take a welcome break.

▽ Poole is still a busy port, but its rail link has gone. In 1976, when it was still active, a Ruston Hornsby shunter belonging to PD Fuels brings empty wagons from the BR exchange sidings.

G.W.R.

Devonport

◁ The town of Poole grew directly from its quayside harbour, and this remained the town's commercial centre until the 1970s This 1920s photograph shows a view of the quay and its railways that was unchanged until relatively recently. In the distance the ovens of the famous pottery can be seen, along with the gantry used for unloading coal.

11 THE QUAY, POOLE

△ An 0-4-0 saddle tank locomotive, No. 4 in the Falmouth Docks Company's fleet, takes empty wagons along the quay in the 1920s.

△ This 1920s card is a reminder that even the smallest ports and harbours had rail connections when possible. Most of the cargoes brought into and out of harbours such as Newquay were essentially local, with coal always high on the necessities list.

▽ Weymouth was famous for its quayside tramway, which connected the harbour to the main station. It was used for passenger services until the 1980s, but in the 1960s, when this photograph was taken, it was also busy with freight, largely to and from the Channel Islands.

THE WEST COUNTRY was always well served with miniature railways, notably at traditional seaside resorts in Devon and Cornwall. A number have been lost, but those that survive tend to be modern in style. Much rarer in this region – quarry lines apart – is the narrow gauge railway. Of these, by far the most important is the much-lamented Lynton & Barnstaple Railway.

"The Jungle Express", Paignton Zoo

WEYMOUTH. MINIATURE RAILWAY

WY 10

◁ Weymouth has had a few miniature lines over the years, including the Weymouth Miniature Railway, whose track ran beside Radipole Lake and below the viaduct that carried the Portland branch line. It operated from 1947 to 1971.

△ Paignton Zoo opened in 1923 and has had a railway since 1937. This 1960s card shows one of the line's individual locomotives, in this case based on a British Railways Warship Class diesel from the Western Region.

▽ Visitors to Newquay have been able to enjoy a short line in Trenance Park for many years. This 1980s card shows old- and new-style motive power, the latter represented by a smart HST 125 power car.

◁ After considerable difficulties the Lynton & Barnstaple
Railway opened its nearly 20-mile line in 1898. The classic nature
of this narrow gauge line is apparent in this 1930s photograph of
a train approaching Woody Bay station.

Lynton and Barnstaple Railway. Woody Bay Station.

◁ Much of the Lynton &
Barnstaple disappeared back
into the Devon landscape after
closure in 1935. This is how
one stretch looked in the 1990s
but, since then, restoration has
brought this section back to life.

△ The Lynton & Barnstaple
published a famous set of Official
Cards in the Edwardian era to
promote its route. These showed
the distinctive style of its
buildings. This is Woody Bay,
which, after a long period as
a house, is now a station again.

△ At Barnstaple Town station
the Lynton & Barnstaple met
the main line, in the form of the
LSWR's branch to Ilfracombe.
In about 1910 a mixed L&B
train, and a dog, wait for the
connecting mainline service.

Barnstaple Town Station.

RAILWAYS APPEARED EARLY in children's books, often for education rather than entertainment, and alphabet and other instructive picture books were popular from the 1860s. Trains featured in books by RM Ballantyne and by Lewis Carroll, and another important book was EE Nesbit's The Railway Children, first published in 1906. The Edwardian era also saw the launch of such large, colourful picture books as The Wonder Book of Trains, which was to go through more than 20 editions before 1950.

Inevitably, the most famous railway books are the Revd W Awdry's Thomas the Tank Engine series, launched in 1945. However, most appealing today, and easily accessible, are the many colour picture books published between the 1920s and the 1960s. Sadly, the artists are rarely identified.

▼ *Engines I Like* was published by Blackie & Son in the late 1930s in their *Untearable* series and contained 16 colour pictures of famous locomotives and trains mounted on board.

▶ Published in the 1950s by Raphael Tuck, *My Book of Trains* contains some dramatic and artistic images of modern British Railways trains, including a diesel-electric express.

MY BOOK OF TRAINS

Raphael Tuck + Sons Ltd   BY APPOINTMENT TO H.M. THE QUEEN FINE ART PUBLISHERS

ENGINES I LIKE

BLACKIE

LIONEL WINS THROUGH

▲ *Lionel Wins Through* is a 1950s boys' adventure story, published in the *Starling* series. The exciting cover, featuring an LNER-style locomotive, is the only illustration.

▶ Another 1950s vision of modern British Railways was published by Collins in their *Wonder Colour Books* series, with pictures by TE North.

Timothy's BOOK OF TRAINS

COLLINS WONDER COLOUR BOOKS

THE GOLDEN PICTURE BOOK OF RAILWAYS

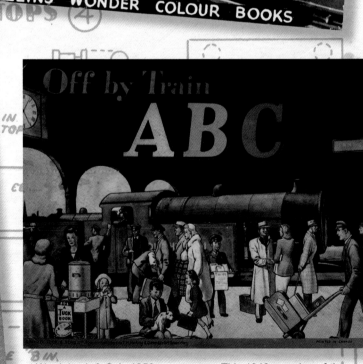

◀ Ward, Lock & Co's 1950s *Golden Picture Book of Railways* has a striking cover and a mass of other pictures.

▲ This 1940s version of the familiar alphabet book was published by Raphael Tuck, with pictures of British trains.

SOUTHERN ENGLAND

THE SEAFORD BRANCH

BY THE LATE 1840s, Lewes was becoming an important railway centre, thanks to the ambitions of the newly formed London, Brighton & South Coast Railway. This company quickly realized the potential of the rather old and decaying port at Newhaven, and in 1847 a 6-mile branch to serve it was opened from Lewes. Cross-channel traffic soon began to flourish, and Newhaven ended up with three stations, Town, Harbour and Marine, the last named being dedicated to boat trains. In 1864 the branch was extended to Seaford. Later the track was doubled and in the 1930s was electrified by the Southern Railway. The branch line lives on today, despite the steady decline of Newhaven harbour.

▽ By the end of the Victorian era Lewes had become the meeting point for six lines, with several London connections. Late-night services from London facilitated theatre excursions, as this handbill indicates.

SOUTHERN RAILWAY.
(2/34) ● TO
Stock 787
LEWES
(L. B. & S. C. Rly.), via COSHAM & HAVANT.

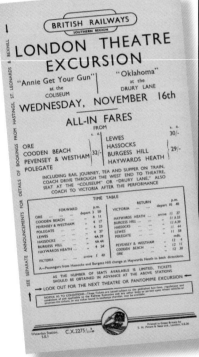

BRITISH RAILWAYS
SOUTHERN REGION
LONDON THEATRE EXCURSION
"Annie Get Your Gun" | "Oklahoma"
at the COLISEUM | at the DRURY LANE
WEDNESDAY, NOVEMBER 16th
ALL-IN FARES

△ This Edwardian view of Lewes gives an idea of how complex the station was in its heyday. The first lines served London and Brighton, with later connections to Seaford, Tunbridge Wells and East Grinstead. The station today is much reduced, and trains for Brighton and Seaford leave from the platforms on the left.

▽ This 1950s view shows Newhaven harbour from the west, with a cross-Channel steamer on its way to the terminal adjacent to Newhaven Marine station.

◁ Newhaven Marine station was, in effect, a short branch off the main line, dedicated to boat trains for cross-Channel services. Over a long period the fastest, most luxurious London–Paris route was via Newhaven and Dieppe. The station was in use until the early 1990s.

▽ In 1950 the Newhaven–Dieppe route was still busy and popular, though it was being gradually eclipsed by services from Dover and Folkestone. Today, a 'No Passport' excursion is inconceivable.

▽ The most remote station on the line is Southease, designed to serve the distant village of Rodmell. Nowadays, more remote than ever and at the end of a lane going nowhere, its survival, together with its 1930s concrete structures, seems extraordinary.

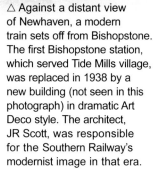

△ Against a distant view of Newhaven, a modern train sets off from Bishopstone. The first Bishopstone station, which served Tide Mills village, was replaced in 1938 by a new building (not seen in this photograph) in dramatic Art Deco style. The architect, JR Scott, was responsible for the Southern Railway's modernist image in that era.

◁ The most famous feature of the landscape east of Seaford is the Seven Sisters, depicted here on a card posted in July 1914 The writer says that Seaford is lovely, little realizing that, soon after his holiday, Europe would be at war.

Seven Sisters Cliffs and Coastguard Station, Seaford.

Bishopstone

377 310   377 310

◁ This card shows Seaford station towards the end of the LB&SC era, busy with holiday and freight traffic. At that time Seaford was a fashionable resort, with a long expanse of beach and plenty of hotels. It was also renowned for its boarding schools. Now housing and car parks have greatly reduced the station site.

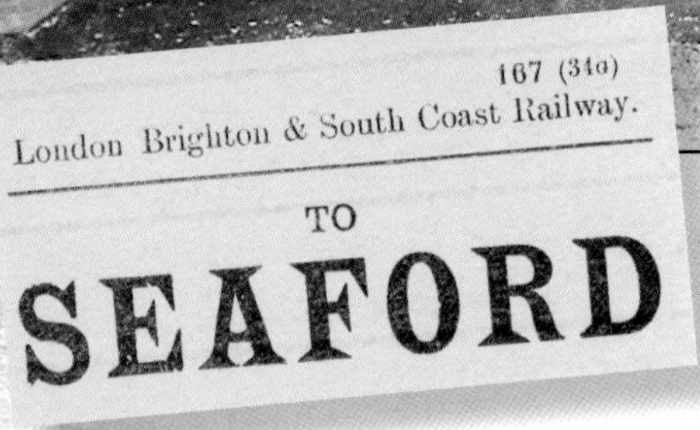

▽ The beach at Seaford, today a rather barren expanse of stones and pebbles, was always popular. Many of the people seen here enjoying the sunshine in July 1908 would have come by train.

London Brighton & South Coast Railway.

167 (310)

TO

SEAFORD

ESPLANADE, LOOKING EAST, SEAFORD.

July 17ᵗ – 08

▽ Seaford station today, although much diminished, retains some of its original 1864 buildings and a particular end-of-the-line atmosphere that is now quite rare in southern England. The Brighton train is ready to depart.

Seaford

377 310   377 310

EPPING TO ONGAR

ALTHOUGH NORMALLY ASSOCIATED with London Transport, the Ongar branch has a long history, stretching back to the 1850s. The Eastern Counties Railway started the process with its branch to Loughton, planning an extension to Epping and Ongar. This was completed in 1865 by the Great Eastern Railway and became part of an expanding suburban network. In the 1930s the LNER began to electrify the route, and by 1949 Central Line tube trains were running to Epping. In 1957 London Transport took over the Ongar branch and made it part of the underground network, where it remained until closure in 1994. There are plans to reopen it.

▷ Despite its proximity to London, Epping retained an air of independence. The nearby forest, described by the writer of this 1981 card as 'lovely at this time of year', was always popular with Londoners.

◁ London Transport worked hard to promote the branch to visitors, as indicated by this 1970s leaflet with its cover picture of the Saxon log church at Greensted.

▽ Between 1949 and 1957 the Ongar branch was worked by elderly LNER tank locomotives and carriages, operating as a push-pull shuttle. This 1953 photograph shows the interchange between London Transport and British Railways at Epping station.

◁ This view of the terminus at Ongar in LNER days shows that it was much more than a basic commuter station. There are extensive freight sidings, a goods shed and an engine shed, and at that time in the pre-London Transport era there were through services to Liverpool Street.

G. E. R.

From _____

TO

ONGAR

▽ Falling traffic and an ageing and complicated single-track route with a level crossing prompted the closure of the branch in 1994. This is London Transport's last timetable for Ongar, issued in July of that year, by which time services were very limited.

◁ The Ongar branch was included as part of the London Transport Underground network from 1957 and was added to the famous map, as seen on this 1963 edition. While a number of Underground stations have been closed over the years, complete line closures have been rare.

▽ A train of modern Central Line tube stock passes through North Weald in the 1980s. By this time Blake Hall, the other intermediate station, was closed. Both had substantial brick buildings in GER style.

Central Line

New edition

ONGAR

From July 1994

THE SELSEY TRAMWAY

THE RATHER EXTRAVAGANTLY NAMED Hundred of Manhood & Selsey Railway was a typical product of the Light Railway Act. Cheaply built and simply operated, the line, just under 8 miles long, ran south from Chichester across an undemanding landscape to Selsey. Opened in August 1897, it was later extended to Selsey Beach. Colonel Stephens was the line's engineer and locomotive superintendent, and he later acquired a controlling interest in the company and added it, renamed as the West Sussex Railway, to his light railway empire. Typically, he operated it with a mixed bag of secondhand carriages and goods vehicles, along with some distinctive locomotives. The first of these, a Peckett-built 2-4-2 tank, was designed by Stephens and named 'Selsey'. The railway closed in 1935. Little survives.

▷ One of the most substantial and interesting remains of the Selsey Tramway is the concrete abutment from the former lifting bridge over the Chichester canal, indentifiable in the old black-and-white photograph (inset, right) showing a train crossing the bridge. This unusual legacy can today be enjoyed by walkers, fishermen and leisure boaters on the canal, now in good condition.

◁ At Chichester, the Selsey Tramway, as it was generally known, had its own rather basic terminus to the south of the mainline station. Here, in about 1915, Manning Wardle locomotive No. 2, 'Sidlesham', waits to haul its two old four-wheel carriages and a box van out of the station.

SOUTHERN RAILWAY.
B. 167 (34G)

Victoria to
SELSEY

▷ At its greatest extent, the Selsey Tramway served 11 stations, including Chichester. Two were private halts, and the remainder were fairly minimal. The station buildings, designed by Colonel Stephens, were simple, corrugated structures, largely prefabricated. Typical was Hunston, the first stop after Chichester.

△ The cable-operated lifting bridge that took trains over the Chichester canal, active when the line was built, was the line's most extraordinary engineering feature, and the slow passage of the train across this rather Heath Robinson structure was the highlight of a journey on this eccentric railway.

▷ When the railway closed in January 1935, much of the infrastructure remained in place. This is Chalder station, some time after closure, with vegetation taking control.

▷ Cheaply built as it was across the flat landscape, the Selsey Tramway has for the most part vanished, but south of Hunston a short stretch survives as footpath.

◁ Few traces of the railway remain today, and exploration is limited. The main survivor is a section south from the site of the Chichester canal bridge, now a footpath in varying states of repair. No buildings survive.

▷ This is Selsey Town station, probably in the late 1920s, with the engine shed on the left. At this point, because road access to Selsey was still quite limited, the railway traffic was adequate, although seasonal.

The Old Cottage, Selsey

◁ The railway's extension to Selsey Beach was short-lived, but it helped Selsey to develop as a popular resort early in the 20th century. While most of the buildings date to that period, there were some older, more historic houses in this remote region, as this Edwardian card indicates.

▽ In its later years the railway was operated by Ford and Shefflex railcars of the kind much favoured by Colonel Stephens. Noisy, smelly and fairly uncomfortable, but cheap to run, they helped to keep the line alive. This is a typical scene at Selsey Town in the early 1930s.

SCRAPBOOK : SOUTHERN ENGLAND

THE DENSITY OF THE RAILWAY NETWORK in the South of England has been a significant element in its long and complex history, formed as it was by fierce competition and the often conflicting demands of freight and commuter traffic. As a result, there were interesting contrasts between the busy main lines radiating from London and the more leisurely cross-country routes, many of which retained their individuality over a long period. There was also a diversity of branch lines, some serving the remote corners of the region. Many of these have inevitably been lost, but their memory survives in photographs and sometimes in physical structures.

▽ In the summer of 1965 the Isle of Wight's highly individual railway network was facing closure. Much of this essentially Victorian railway had already gone, but still alive were the lines from Ryde to Newport, Cowes and Ventnor. Part of this, remarkably, was destined to be saved and reborn, including Ryde Pier Head station, where the driver and his locomotive, No. 33 'Bembridge', pose in the sunshine.

◁ A typically remote corner of the network was served by the Lee-on-the-Solent Light Railway, whose short line to Fort Brockhurst opened in 1894. Never a success, it was operated for some years by the contractor who built it before being taken over by the LSWR in 1909. It crept into the Southern Railway's empire, and was closed in 1931. This photograph, probably taken around the time of the closure, wonderfully captures the sense of inactivity that must always have prevailed on this obscure branch line.

▽ ◁ The first railway route to Portsmouth actually went to Gosport, with a ferry connection. This was opened in 1841, with an unusually grand terminus station in the classical style designed by Sir William Tite. In 1845 the line was extended to the Royal Victoria station, used by the royal family on journeys to and from the Isle of Wight. The direct route to Portsmouth opened in 1847, but Gosport continued to receive passengers until 1953. Goods traffic survived until 1969. Today the station is a magnificent ruin, looking like something that belongs in Rome rather than Hampshire.

▷ A typical cross-country route was Redhill to Guildford and Reading. It was never electrified, and steam lingered on into the 1960s. Here, with a bridge at Deepdene under reconstruction, an old N Class locomotive, No. 31831, crawls its train across, while a smart new MGA passes underneath.

▽ Penshurst in Kent, one of the quieter stations on the Tonbridge-to-Guildford route, is the setting for this smoky scene. In March 1960 an ancient C Class 0-6-0 locomotive, No. 31724, eeks out its last years on maintenance duties as it hurries a ballast-cleaning special through the station.

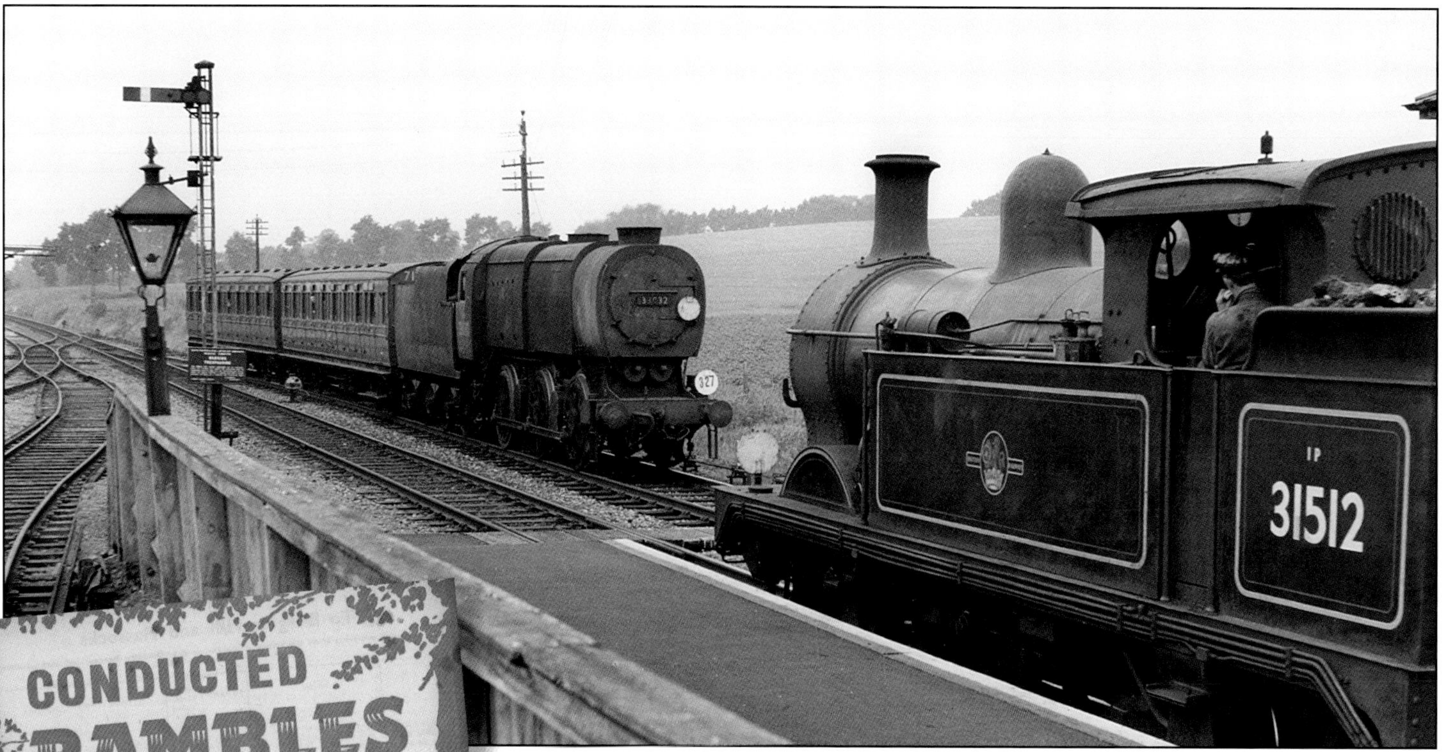

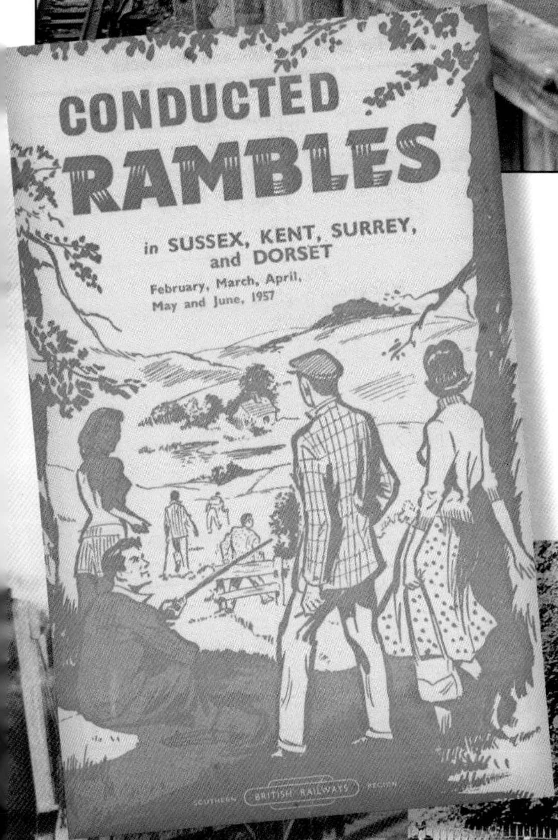

CONDUCTED RAMBLES
in SUSSEX, KENT, SURREY, and DORSET
February, March, April, May and June, 1957

△ Passenger services on the Allhallows-on-Sea branch from Gravesend ended in 1961. The line, which survives in part for the Isle of Grain oil terminal, had seen better days, with cross-Channel services from Port Victoria. This is Sharnal Street station in 1960, with closure on the horizon.

▽ Schoolboys on their bikes have gathered to examine the scene of an 'incident' at Horsham on 30 May 1957. An old C2X Class 0-6-0 locomotive has failed to stop, driving the buffers firmly into the wall of the bridge. Driver error, perhaps? The locomotive seems to have survived, as it was still listed in the Ian Allan 'ABC' book in 1958. Curiously, the photograph was issued by the British Railways Public Relations Department at Waterloo, who might have wanted to keep such things quiet.

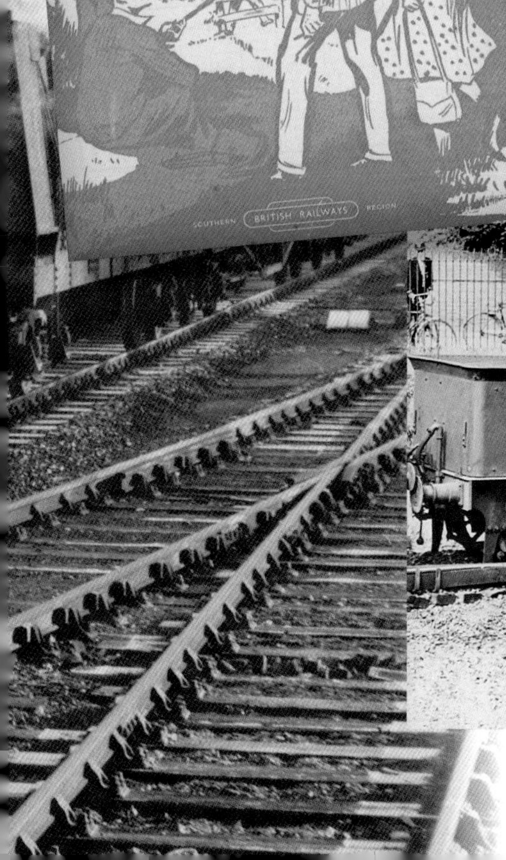

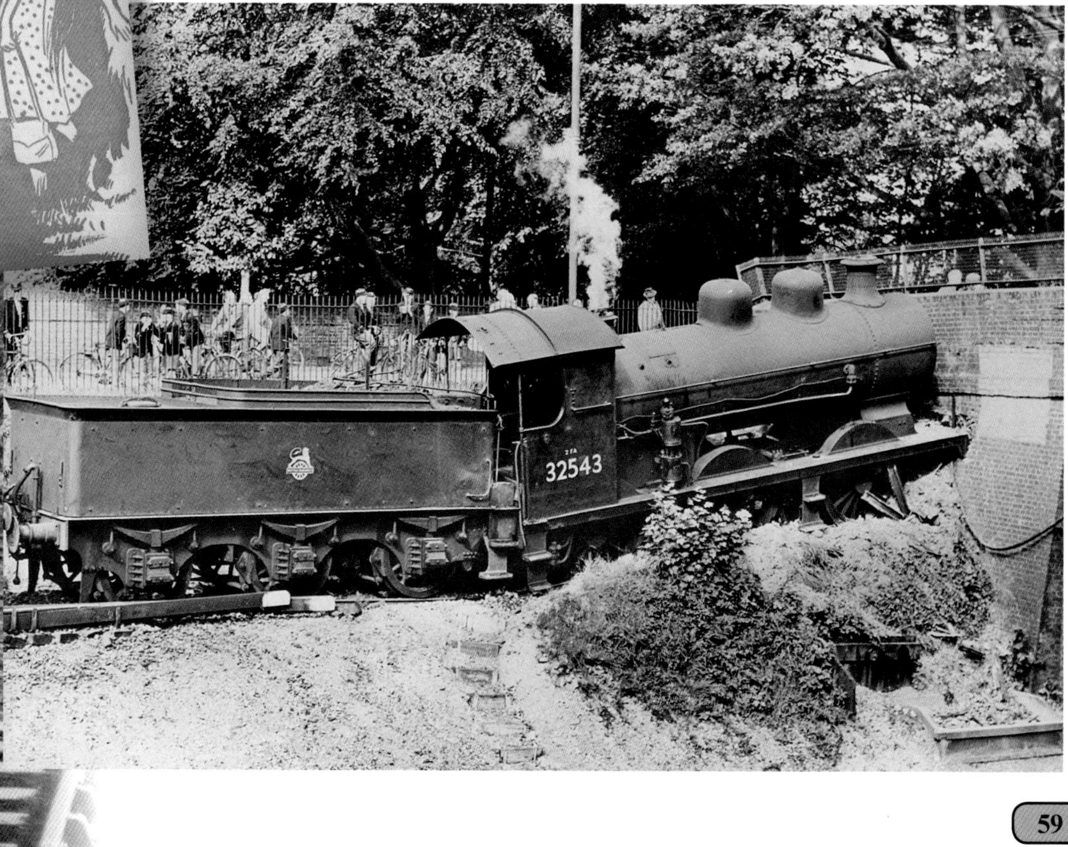

△ Staines was firmly in LSWR territory, but the GWR managed to edge in from the north with a branch from West Drayton. This is their terminus at Staines West on a quiet day in 1953. The line closed in March 1965.

▽ London's underground railways started with steam haulage in 1863 and, surprisingly, steam lasted on the London Transport network until 1971 – longer than on British Railways. In their last years, the steam locomotives were used for maintenance duties and, inevitably, there were many steam specials. Here, watched by two young children, L44 rests while on an LRPS special. This locomotive, built for the Metropolitan Railway in 1898, was withdrawn in 1963.

◁ This minimal station is Poyle Estate Halt, on the GWR's Staines West branch, seen on the day of closure, 29 March 1965. Someone has already removed one of the totem name signs!

▷ The transport of hop-pickers to the hop fields in Kent was a major railway business for decades. It was still going strong in the 1950s, when this handbill was printed, but has long been extinct.

▽ In June 1961 the normally busy Westbourne Park Road in west London was disrupted by the passage of the famous GWR locomotive 'Caerphilly Castle', here being eased round a corner on its Pickfords low-loader. The first of its class in 1923, and probably always scheduled for preservation, 'Caerphilly Castle' now resides at STEAM Museum of the Great Western Railway, in Swindon.

THE POST OFFICE RAILWAY

A stretch of experimental atmospheric railway to carry mail beneath the streets of London was operated briefly in the 1870s, but the Post Office Railway was much more substantial. Constructed from 1914 and opened for traffic in 1927, this 6-mile-long underground railway ran in a 9ft-diameter tunnel from Paddington to Whitechapel via intermediate stops, mostly main sorting offices. The locomotive-hauled trains were completely automatic, controlled from switch cabins at five stations. Designed to speed distribution of mail and to reduce traffic on the streets of London, the trains at their peak carried over 45,000 mail bags per day.

Post Office Railway

GPO COMMEMORATIVE COVER

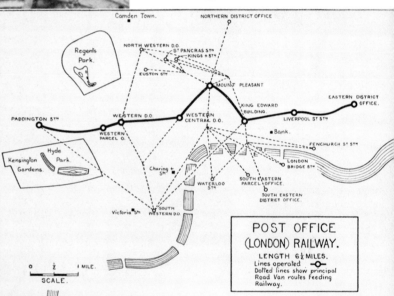

▲ This map shows the route of the Post Office Railway across London and the six intermediate stations between Paddington station and the Eastern District Office at Whitechapel, with their road connections. Each station had a platform and two tracks, for stopping and non-stopping trains.

◀ The tunnel for the Post Office Railway was bored 80ft below the streets of London. It carried two tracks, with a third rail for the power supply, and up to 40 trains an hour could use the system. This shows one of the driverless, remote-controlled locomotives and its single-car container train. The railway was abandoned in 2003 – an act of madness that put all the traffic back onto the roads – but the tunnels are still there.

▶ The switch cabin at Mount Pleasant Sorting Office, shown here, controlled trains on the section that passed through the largest and most complex station on the railway.

◀ ▼ The Post Office Railway was unique in the world, and the 40th and 50th anniversaries of its opening in 1927 were suitably celebrated with commemorative First Day Covers.

▶ This shows the railway's main depot and workshop, with full maintenance facilities. Battery-powered locomotives were held in readiness to deal with faulty trains or for track maintenance when the power was turned off.

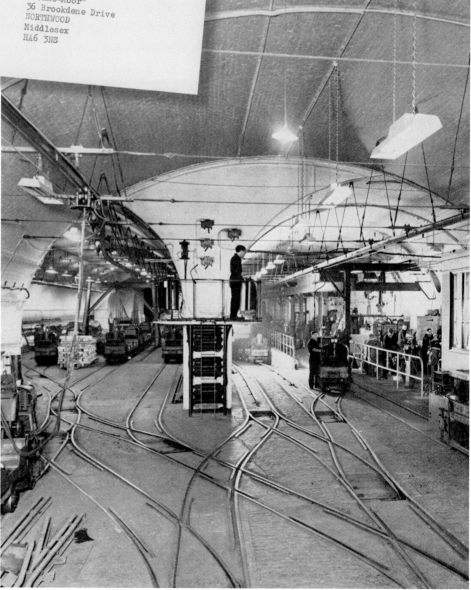

▲ After sorting, the mail bags were put onto containers to be loaded in sets of four directly onto the railway wagons. The system was highly mechanized.

THE EAST KENT RAILWAY

THE KENT COALFIELD, now consigned to history, was discovered during the trial boring for the proposed Channel Tunnel in 1882. A number of collieries were subsequently opened in the area, the main one being at Tilmanstone. In 1910 the East Kent Railway was launched to serve these collieries, and from 1911 its line was gradually built northwards from Shepherdswell towards Wingham, reached by 1916. The same year, passenger-carrying started, and a branch was built to serve a new World War I port at Richborough, near Sandwich, also busy in World War II. A planned extension to Canterbury ended in 1925 at Canterbury Road, just beyond Wingham. The line's engineer, and later its owner, was Colonel Stephens. Coal remained the primary traffic. After years of uncertain operation, closures began in 1948. By 1951 only the branch serving Tilmanstone colliery was open. This survived until the whole Kent coalfield was obliterated in the 1980s.

▷ The East Kent Railway, though linked to the main line at Shepherdswell, started from its own station, a one-platform affair set in a cutting to the north. The small white building partly visible on the right was the ticket office. Coaching stock was mixed, as seen here,

▽ This 1931 view shows Shepherdswell station from the other direction, with the tracks leading to the goods yard and carriage sidings on the right. Here there was an engine shed and the linking spur to the main line. When the railway was opened, this was the SE&CR, later the Southern.

◁ There were several level crossings along the route, generally ungated, reflective of the rather eccentric and hand-to-mouth operation of the railway. It was built as a coal line, but a number of the pits it was designed to serve were never completed or, if they were, proved uneconomic. By default, passenger and general goods traffic therefore became the mainstay of the line.

▽ North of Eythorne all lines were closed in 1951 and then lifted. The East Kent was a lightly engineered railway, so much of its route has disappeared back into the landscape. Traces can be found, notably low embankments in a few places. More visible is the route of the line that continued to serve Tilmanstone colliery until the 1980s, such as this section near Eythorne.

◁ Apart from Golgotha tunnel, just north of Shepherdswell, the railway's major engineering feature was the bridge that carried the Richborough branch over a road, a river and the main line to Deal. Today, only the brick piers survive, with part of the approach embankment.

▽ The bridge looks like a primitive steel girder structure, yet it carried heavy traffic during both world wars, when Richborough was a major cross-Channel supply port.

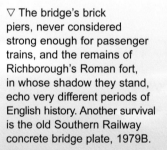

▽ The bridge's brick piers, never considered strong enough for passenger trains, and the remains of Richborough's Roman fort, in whose shadow they stand, echo very different periods of English history. Another survival is the old Southern Railway concrete bridge plate, 1979B.

◁ The East Kent was a light railway, and its trains had to stay within the 25mph speed limit – which was probably just as well, considering the state of some of the track. There was never a major accident, but derailments, mostly of goods wagons, were not uncommon.

▷ In its heyday, the East Kent had a considerable local network, linking collieries and Richborough, and serving mostly small agricultural communities via its 16 stations. Apart from those on the main line, there were three stations on the first section of the Richborough branch after Eastry Junction, though Richborough itself was never served by passenger trains. Most stations were very basic. This is Knowlton, seen here shortly before closure. It served a church, a farm and a few cottages.

△ Passenger services over the whole route, from Shepherdswell to Wingham and Canterbury Road, were scheduled but infrequent, and towards the end there were only two a day. Many passenger trains also included goods wagons. Here at Eythorne in the 1920s, a surprising number of passengers are waiting for their train.

▷ In its latter years, before the advent of diesels in 1961, the coal trains were operated by a small fleet of Class 01 locomotives dating from the 1890s. This is 31065, the last survivor of its class, hauling a coal train in the summer of 1959 near Golgotha tunnel. Today, the preserved East Kent Railway operates trains on a reopened section between Shepherdswell and Eythorne.

▽ Wingham was in reality the end of the line, although construction did start on an extension to Canterbury. This came to an end in 1925 in a field 6 miles east of Canterbury, at a little station optimistically called Canterbury Road. Today, the Railway Station Farm Shop occupies the site of Wingham Town station, while the station pictured here, although the nameboard says simply Wingham, is Wingham Canterbury Road.

◁ The railway was built to serve several collieries in the area, including Guilford, which was connected via a branch line from near Tilmanstone. Opened in 1912, this never fulfilled its promise and was soon closed. The route is now almost impossible to trace, but some of the Guilford mine buildings survive, including this substantial winding house, now in private use.

▽ The Kent coalfield was destroyed after the coal strike of 1984, so little remains of this important part of Kent's industrial history. However, clues can be found, including this signpost near Eythorne.

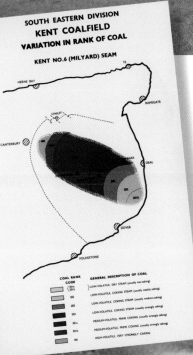

◁ This National Coal Board survey map from 1959 shows the location and quality of the Kent coalfield. Its three main centres were Tilmanstone, Betteshanger and Snowdown. The latter two were directly connected to mainline railways.

△ Tilmanstone, photographed here in the 1920s, was a massive enterprise and the major colliery in the region. It was the principal reason for the building of the East Kent Railway, and it remained the primary user of the line until its closure in 1986.

GENERAL GOODS

THE DENSE RAILWAY NETWORK of southern England has always reflected its primary purpose, namely short-distance passenger carrying, so there are fewer industrial lines here than in other parts of the country. Quarries, brickworks, oil terminals and docks have generated some traffic, even in the South, but more significant have been factories, supply depots and industrial installations with dedicated sidings, networks and mainline connections. Many of these were built to serve the needs of London, including gas works, power stations and waste-disposal plants and, until the latter part of the 20th century, particularly during the era when coal was king, most were rail-operated. Now, the traffic is dominated by container and bulk-cargo trains.

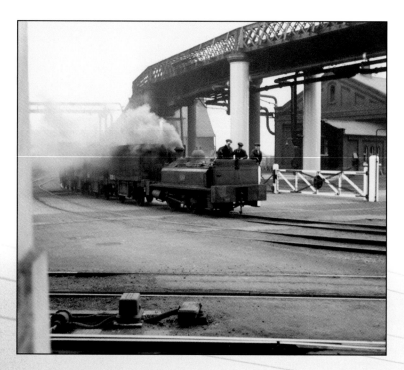

◁ Beckton gas works in East London had an extensive railway network to bring in the coal and remove the coke that was the byproduct of the gas-making process. Locomotives used here, and at other gas plants, were specially built with a low profile, to enable them to pass under the gas retorts.

▽ By 1969 steam had disappeared from the British Rail network but it lingered on in numerous industrial sites. London Transport was still using steam for its maintenance trains and for hauling rubbish to the Watford waste-disposal site. In February of that year, L90, a former GWR pannier tank locomotive, makes plenty of smoke as it crosses the Grand Union Canal on the way back from Watford.

▽ In the summer of 1972 aggregate traffic was still flowing on the Lavant branch north from Chichester, the truncated remains of the former cross-country route to Midhurst. Here, diesel locomotive 6569 takes a heavy train away from the Lavant quarry site. Today the track has gone and the former route is a footpath.

▷ John Parish started supplying sand ballast to ships on the Thames in 1805, using sand pits near Erith. A 4ft gauge railway, steam-hauled from the 1860s, operated the traffic. This photograph, perhaps from the 1920s, shows the railway and a typical 0-4-0 saddle tank locomotive. The line closed in 1957.

▽ In the 1960s 'Benton II', a well-cared-for 0-4-0 industrial locomotive belonging to timber-merchants Burt, Boulton & Haywood Ltd, rests on siding at Totton, near Southampton.

△ In the 1970s factories and industrial sites all over Britain were still rail-connected, via sidings that often crossed roads. Here, in June 1973, a Class 08 diesel shunter pushes some open wagons over Green Lane and into the Woolwich yard of Standard Telephones and Cables. The Stratford-to-Woolwich line is on the right.

PORTS & HARBOURS OF SOUTHERN ENGLAND

SMALL HARBOURS AND DOCKS, mostly sited by river estuaries, have been a feature of southern England at least since Roman times. Some, famous in the medieval era, have disappeared; others, largely in response to the demands of industry, shipping and the railways, have come to prominence.

From the late 19th century the railway-owned and operated cross-Channel ports rose in importance. Traffic greatly increased in World War I, notably at Southampton, which became a major international enterprise in the Southern Railway era. At the same time, smaller, more specialized ports also flourished.

◁ Even small docks and harbours usually had a railway connection, while larger ones were served by complex networks. It was not unusual to see road and rail side by side. This is Dover in the 1920s.

▷ The *Queen Mary* was a popular icon, and thousands gathered in May 1936 to see her depart from Southampton on her maiden voyage to New York. The special excursion promoted here was to see her return, on 10 June 1936.

WELCOME
R.M.S.
"QUEEN MARY"
HOME

WEDNESDAY, JUNE 10th.

SPECIAL RAIL & STEAMER
EXCURSION (via PORTSMOUTH)

SOUTHERN RAILWAY

G. W. R.

SOUTHAMPTON DOCKS

▷ In the 1920s and 1930s the Southern Railway turned Southampton into one of the greatest docks in the world. In the 1960s, when this view was published, it was still largely railway-operated.

▷ Some harbours were dedicated to specialized traffic. At Ridham Dock, to the north of Sittingbourne, materials for papermaking were unloaded and transported to mills at Sittingbourne and Kemsley via a narrow gauge network opened from 1906. This shows shunting at Ridham dock in 1961.

△ Operated for much of its life by Bowaters, this narrow gauge line is now preserved. It had a famous fleet of locomotives, some dating back to the start of the railway. This is 'Superior', a Kerr Stuart 0-6-2, seen at Kemsley in 1969.

London Brighton & South Coast Railway.

Newhaven Harbour to
Portsm'th Har.

Boulogne Steamer getting ready to sail.   Folkestone.

△ Places such as Folkestone and Dover are now regarded as passenger and vehicle ports, but in the late Victorian era their growth was more closely linked to freight. This card shows an early form of container being loaded at Folkestone onto a ferry bound for Boulogne.

◁ Quayside railways were a feature of most docks and harbours, at least until the 1960s. Here, in the 1930s, an 0-6-0 dock shunter and its crew take a rest between duties at a small harbour in the Southern Railway's network.

THE MOST FAMOUS NARROW GAUGE railway in southern England, the Romney, Hythe & Dymchurch, is really a miniature line, but the length of its route and its history has given it a status well beyond its 15in gauge. There were a few genuine narrow gauge lines built for passenger carrying, two of which are shown here, but the majority were for industrial or quarry use.

▷ This decorative First Day Cover was issued in January 1978 to mark 21 years of British nuclear energy and to celebrate 50 years of the Romney, Hythe & Dymchurch line. The covers were posted at Dungeness nuclear power station and were then carried on the coal-powered railway.

R.H.D.R. and
Dungeness Power S
Official

RHDR COVER No. 4

▷ Opened in 1883, Volk's Electric Railway was a sensation in Edwardian Brighton, as this card indicates. It was Britain's first electric railway, and its route along the beach and promenade is still in use.

▽ The Rye & Camber Tramway, a typically quirky tourist railway, was opened in 1895 and extended to Camber Sands, seen here, in 1908. After heavy use by the Admiralty in World War II, it was sold for scrap in 1947.

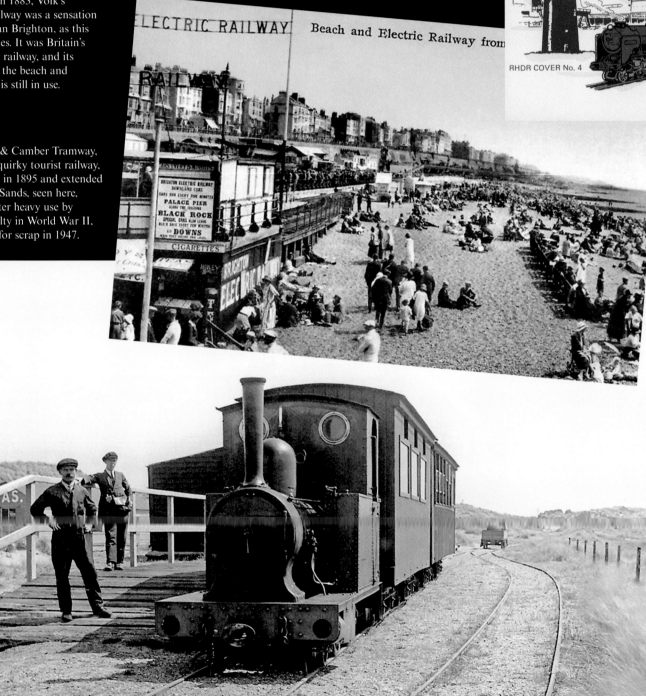

△ In August 1939 Auntie Rosie sent this card to her nephew Michael in Bath and described her ride on a train hauled by the locomotive 'Dr Syn', pictured top right on the card.

▷ The RH&DR has always been publicity-conscious, and its wide range of promotional and souvenir material included from the early days a series of coloured postcards featuring scenes on the line and its famous locomotives. This card, No. 22 in the series, shows 'Typhoon' beside the LNER's famous 'Flying Scotsman', upon which it was based. Photographs suggest that this 'meeting' actually took place, unlikely though it seems.

◁ This delightful 1950s card is typical of the hundreds produced by, for or about the RH&DR. Only the horse gives away the small scale of the train.

THE SOUTH COAST OF ENGLAND could perhaps be described as a line of resorts, so it is not surprising that miniature railways have long been a feature of the region, with at least 20 operating at one time or another between Poole and the Thames estuary. In addition, there were a number of famous inland lines, notably at Camberley, in Surrey, and in London's Battersea Park during the Festival of Britain.

THE SURREY BORDER & CAMBERLEY RAILWAY

△ Opened in 1938, the Surrey Border & Camberley Railway in Surrey was justly famous, although short-lived. Running from Blackwater, near Camberley, to Farnborough Green, it was built on a grand scale. It closed in September 1939, but some of its locomotives lived on elsewhere.

NO. 14. SOUTHSEA MINIATURE RAILWAY.

△ Southsea's first line opened in 1924 and is seen here in the 1930s. Since then there have been three more, with varied gauges and locomotives. The last was transferred to Netley in 1989.

▷ Despite strong winds, it is a busy day in the 1950s on the Littlehampton miniature railway. It was opened in 1948, from the common to Mewsbrook Park.

MINIATURE TRAIN AND THE COMMON, SOUTH HAYLING, HAYLING ISLAND, K.3288.

MINIATURE RAILWAY, LITTLEHAMPTON

△ This card shows Hayling Island's first line, opened in the 1930s, with one of the original locomotives. Since then, this and two other lines have closed, but there is one operating today.

PLEASE HELP   THE HORSES

27 YEAR OLD HONEY COLLECTING FARES   MEADOW END RAILWAY, BROCKENHURST

◁ New Forest ponies were a feature of Meadow End Railway near Brockenhurst, Hampshire, and these 1950s children are enjoying the close-up experience.

△ Southern Miniature Railways operated lines from the late 1940s in Southsea, Bognor Regis and Poole, seen here in the 1960s with the locomotive 'Vanguard' making the circuit of the lake.

▽ Since 1920 Margate has had several miniature railways. This 1950s card shows the one that operated by the old stone pier from 1947 to 1964, with its locomotive of the 'Flying Scotsman' type.

▷ This is 'Neptune', the locomotive used on the Far Tottering & Oyster Creek Railway, a charmingly eccentric line designed by Rowland Emmett for the Festival of Britain in Battersea Park in 1951.

▽ Bognor Regis is a famous name in miniature railway history. Its first line opened in 1909 and is seen here with locomotive 'Winnie'. It did not last long, but the resort has since enjoyed at least five other railways in various locations, including Hotham Park, Butlin's and the pier.

TOY TRAINS

THE RAILWAY EXPERIENCE became increasingly accessible and familiar from the 1840s. Images of locomotives and trains began to feature on children's pottery and in children's books in the same period, and by the 1850s toy trains were being made in quantity, notably in Germany and America. These were simple toys in metal or wood, designed to run on the carpet or the floor rather than on rails, and there was little attempt to make them accurate as models. Toy trains did not then change significantly until the latter part of the Victorian era, when the first train sets and scale models began to appear, again mostly from German manufacturers. In the first decades of the 20th century, the business expanded massively with the emergence of familiar names such as Bassett-Lowke and Hornby, and this set the pattern for the future.

▼ Photographers started to pose children with toys – some of them no doubt props – in the 1850s. This young boy was probably photographed at about that time, to judge by the style of the chair and the early toy train he is clutching in his hand.

For Your FIFTH BIRTHDAY.
Take a message true from me
That you may very happy be,
And find that your 5th Birthday brings
All the very Jolliest things.

A5·2.

▼ There must be thousands of cards celebrating the theme of children and their love of trains. The 1950s example shown below reflects every boy's ambition of becoming an engine driver.

I am Driving a Train and Going Full Steam Ahead.

▲ Numerical birthday cards were made in the Victorian period. This early 1930s card for a boy features a Hornby 0 gauge train set.

▲ This charming 1920s photograph features Albert with his toy locomotive, probably an amateur production made by a relative using left-over bits of wood. Commercially made equivalents were available.

Playcraft RAILWAYS

"LAKESIDE"
COMBINATION RAILWAY LAYOUT

Here in one handy storage box you will find all the add[...]
Track and Accessories (listed below) you require to ma[...]
really exciting layout, plus a beautifully printed plan in full[...]
showing all landscape details, ready for permanent moun[...]
a base board 34" × 48".

Contains: 2 P.4700 Curved Rails; 3 P.4702 Curved Half Rails; 2 P.4[...]
R.H.; 2 P.4045 Point L.H.; 2 P.4752 Straight Rail; 1 P.480 Uncou[...]
2 P.478 Buffer Rail; 1 P.4750 Straight Rail; 1 P.7205 Goods Shed/Co[...]
form; 1 P.675 Level Crossing; 1 P.710 Island Platform and 16 Traveling[...]
Re-railer Track; 1 P.680 Tunnel; 1 P.683 Signals Kit; 1 P.684 Teleg[...]
(10 per box); 1 P.685 Fences (8 per box); 1 P.682 Trackside Ind[...]
1 P.892 3-speed Reversing Battery Control Unit; 1 P.614 Printed L[...]
P.1580   All above items plus GOO[...]
P.1350 as listed.
P.1501   All above items plus P[...]
TRAIN P.1450 as listed.

Space required for layou[...]

24   Printed in Great Britain

▲ The Playcraft range of electric 00 gauge railways was basic but extensive, and reasonably accurate. Aimed at children rather than their parents, the models were made from plastic. This 1960s catalogue includes British and French ranges.

▶ A 1930s schoolboy holds his 0 gauge model, perhaps made by Bassett-Lowke, while it is oiled by the driver of the real thing. 'The London Irish Rifleman' was an LMS Royal Scot locomotive built in 1927 and originally numbered 6138.

▼ This 1930s postcard explores a birthday or Christmas scenario familiar to many families.

"Thanks so much for giving me that lovely present, Dad."

1955/6   U.K.

HORNBY
Clockwork
TRAINS
Gauge 'O'

The prices in this folder are cancelled. Ask for revised price list.

MADE IN ENGLAND BY MECCANO LTD.

Prices include Purchase Tax where applicable

HT/CF/1

▲ Most 20th-century British boys dreamed of owning a Hornby train set, starting usually with something from the 0 gauge clockwork range. This is the catalogue for 1955/6.

79

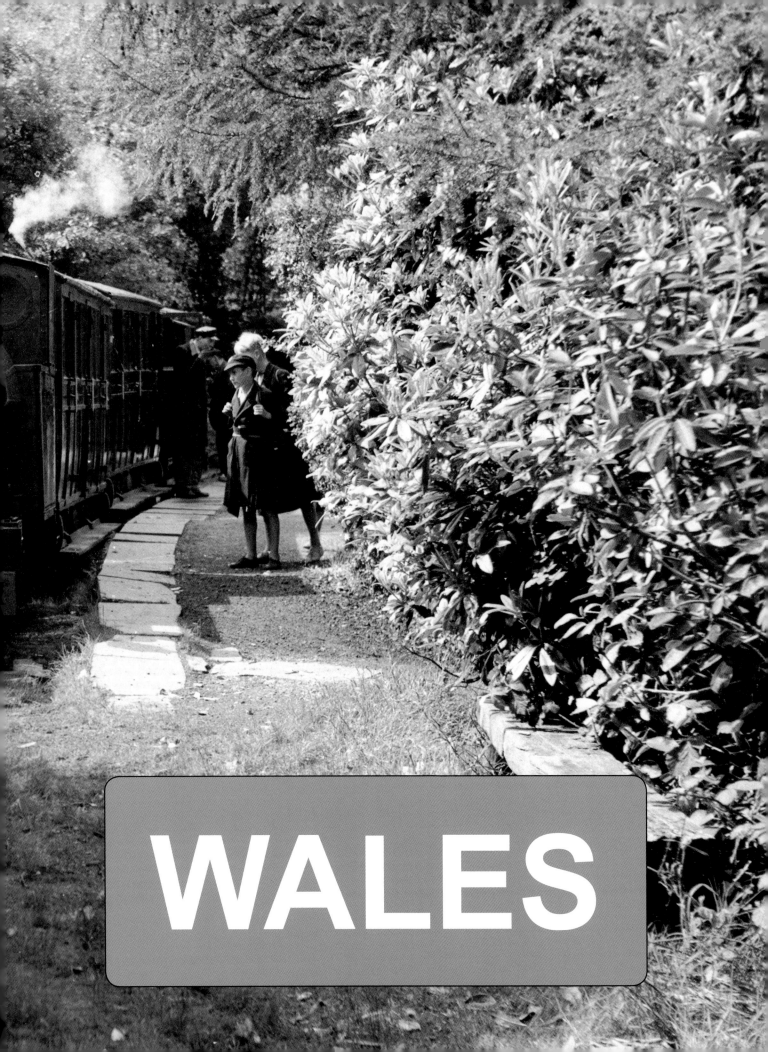

WALES

THE EBBW VALE BRANCH

THE RAILWAY NETWORK of the South Wales Valleys north of Cardiff was, at its peak, dense and confusing. Ebbw Vale was not alone in having two stations. The first, on a line north from Newport, was built by the Monmouthshire Railway and opened in 1855. It was primarily a freight line, but passenger services continued until 1962. Between then and 2001, when the Corus steelworks closed, coal and steel traffic kept the line open, by which time pressure was mounting to reopen it for passenger services. Welsh devolution helped the campaign, and in February 2008 trains returned to this famous valley line.

▽ The scenic quality of the reopened Ebbw Vale branch is apparent in this photograph, taken near Risca in February 2008. It is hoped that the line, as well as helping the local economy, will encourage tourism. It is interesting that reopenings are actively supported by regional governments in Wales and Scotland, while little happens in England.

◁ Passenger services ceased in 1962, and in April of that year an old ex-GWR pannier tank locomotive, No. 8786, takes its short train away from Aberbeeg and the junction with lines to Bryn-mawr and Abergavenny, towards Ebbw Vale. Passenger trains were soon to disappear from all the lines in this area.

▽ Iron and steel were part of the history of Ebbw Vale for decades. In the 1920s, when this advertisement appeared in a railway magazine, these industries were vital to the economy of the region. Steel-making finally ended in Ebbw Vale in 2001.

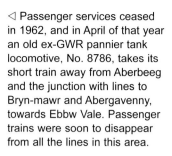

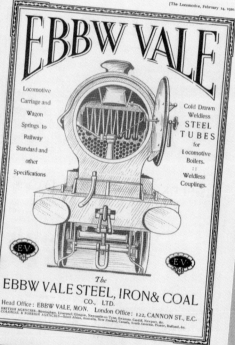

▽ Risca station, seen below in the late 1950s, was close to an important junction with the line to Tredegar. The modern photograph to the left was taken near the site. Nothing of the original station remains, and there is a new one, called Risca and Pontymister, a little to the south.

△ For over 45 years the Ebbw Vale line was kept open by freight traffic, largely serving the local steel works. Here, in 1988, a Class 37 diesel hauls a line of empty steel wagons southwards between Aberbeeg and Llanhilleth.

G. W. R.

Ebbw Vale

▷ Ebbw Vale originally had two stations, the legacy of fierce competition between railway companies in the 19th century. This is the Low Level station, on the line from Newport, while High Level was at the end of a short branch from the Abergavenny line.

▷ By 1962, DMU railcars were in use on the line, in a last-ditch attempt at keeping it open by cutting costs and improving efficiency. However, it was in vain, and closure was imminent. The reopened line currently terminates at Ebbw Vale Parkway, well to the south, but will be extended to Ebbw Vale, though not to the station photographed here.

▽ The newly reopened line runs from Ebbw Vale Parkway to Cardiff, rather than Newport. A connection to Newport may come later, along with a link to Abertillery. The first passenger trains back on the line were Class 150 units, one of which is seen here near Cwm.

2nd-SINGLE SINGLE-2nd
Ebbw Vale to
Ebbw Vale Ebbw Vale
VictoriaMon VictoriaMon
VICTORIA (MON.)
(W) 5d Fare 5d (W)
For conditions see over For conditions see over
5484

THE HOLYWELL BRANCH

HOLYWELL TAKES ITS NAME from the Well of St Winefride, an early Christian martyr beheaded by Prince Caradoc after she had refused his advances. The well, fed by a natural spring, has a long history as a place of pilgrimage, and as late as 1870 a new hospice was built to cater for the pilgrims' needs. The coming of the railway, a private venture by the Holywell Railway Company, was probably linked to that. It opened in 1867, its short but heavily graded 2-mile route following an earlier tramway to the Dee estuary. Commercially unsuccessful, this railway was abandoned in the 1870s. About 30 years later it was rescued and bought by the LNWR, reopening

to passengers and goods in July 1913. The company worked hard to make it into a successful tourist line, replacing the bus service it had introduced in 1905. Local textile mills also generated traffic, and this survived until 1957, when the line was finally closed. Passenger services stopped running in 1954, at which point there were still about 20 trains on weekdays.

▽ The Chester & Holyhead Railway was an important part of an early trunk route. George Stephenson was the engineer, and he made his mark on the line's structures and buildings. Holywell Junction station, designed by Francis Thompson and completed in 1848, was strikingly elegant, looking more like an Italianate villa than a station. Closed in 1966, it survives as a private house, overlooking its abandoned platforms and the busy North Wales line, seen here with a passing mineral train and a distant view of an old ship moored in the estuary. This grand station was the starting point for the short journey to Holywell Town.

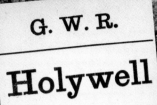

△ ▷ The photograph above shows the neatly manicured site of Holywell Town station, with few clues to its past. The trackbed is a footpath, and the old stone bridge seems far older than the railway age that created it. Yet the 1920s view to the right shows the same bridge, spanning the end of the steep branch and the minimal station that served Holywell.

△ In 1905 the LNWR, keen to promote traffic to Holywell, started a bus service from the mainline station. This detail from an LNWR Official Card celebrates this service. It was replaced by the opening of the railway in 1913.

▷ The veneration of St Winefride prompted the building of a chapel in 1480 by the mother of King Henry VII. The actual spring was fed into a cistern in the chapel's crypt. This Edwardian card shows the chapel, and indicates that the popularity of the pilgrimage site continued well into the 20th century.

HOLYWELL. ST. WINIFREDS WELL

THE DYSERTH BRANCH

IN 1869 THE LNWR OPENED a short branch from Prestatyn to Dyserth to serve local mines and quarries, one of a number of mineral lines in the North Wales region. The rise of tourism during the late 1800s prompted the LNWR to introduce passenger services on the branch from 1905, and these continued to operate until September 1930. A feature of the line were the steam railmotors, or railcars, used for the passenger services, depicted in a series of postcards issued to mark their introduction.

The line remained open for freight traffic until 1973. After closure, the trackbed was converted into a walkway and cycleway. This is now the start of the North Wales Path, which continues to Bangor.

△ This 1920s postcard shows Meliden and the line curving along the valley, below Fish Mountain. The station is in the bottom lefthand corner. The large, modern photograph at the bottom of this page shows the same scene from a more distant viewpoint.

◁ Smartly dressed Edwardian visitors admire the Dyserth waterfall, one of a number of attractions in the region that encouraged the LNWR to introduce passenger services on the Dyserth branch in 1905.

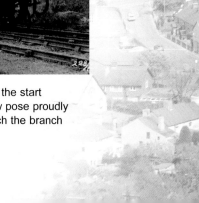

△ This is one of a series of cards produced to mark the start of passenger services on the branch. Here, the crew pose proudly by their vehicle, one of the steam railmotors for which the branch was famous.

◁ The walkway along the trackbed of the branch is well hidden in the landscape and protected from encroaching development. The route is punctuated by a number of bridges in stone and brick. The largest, a viaduct, is now a listed structure.

▷ The site of the former station at Meliden is marked by buildings and the remains of a loading gauge, a reminder that for much of its life the Dyserth branch was primarily a mineral line.

▽ This panoramic view, taken from the summit of Graig Fawr, shows Prestatyn and the coast in the distance, with Meliden in the foreground. The curving, tree-lined walkway runs across the open landscape in the centre right of the photograph.

LEOMINSTER TO NEW RADNOR & PRESTEIGN

THE EARLY DECADES of the railway age were filled with schemes destined to be unfulfilled. A typical example was a plan for a line westwards from Leominster, in Herefordshire, across Wales towards Aberystwyth. This started as the Leominster & Kington Railway, whose 13-mile line was opened in 1857. Nothing further happened until the 1870s, when two branch lines were added, from Titley to Presteign (or Presteigne) and from Kington to New Radnor, the latter making some use of an earlier mineral tramway.

Another line went southwards from Titley to Talyllyn Junction via Hay-on-Wye. This whole network became part of the GWR in the 1890s. Never busy, the lines closed progressively from 1951, with the first casualties being the branches to New Radnor and Presteign. At that point Presteign was served by two trains a day, with an extra one on Saturdays. Freight lived on into the mid-1960s.

△ Even remote stations like New Radnor were a source of local pride, and important to the local economy, as this Edwardian view indicates.

△ Opened in 1853 by the Shrewsbury & Hereford Railway, Leominster's brick-and-stone station had at its peak four platforms and a tall signal box, visible in the distance on this old photograph. Some buildings survive, though the station is much reduced in size.

▽ New Radnor's station survives, somewhat the worse for wear and rather isolated in a mobile home park.

G. W. R.

NEW RADNOR

▽ Much of the route of this local network can still be traced and explored. Bridges survive, such as this example near Titley, now in a delightfully sylvan setting.

▷ Today, Titley Junction station is a private house. It has retained much of its original quality, and rescued railway vehicles and artefacts help to underline the history.

△ In the interwar period Titley Junction, though never very busy, was well looked after, with all the qualities of a rural GWR station. This was the starting point for the Presteign branch.

△ By 1964 Titley Junction was disused and overgrown, though track and station signboard were still present. The old ganger's trolley emphasizes the sense of decay.

▷ It is the summer of 1964 and closure is imminent. The occasional pick-up goods still runs, and here, at Bullock Mill crossing, near Kington, the guard closes the gates while the train waits.

G.W.R.

Kington

PRESTEIGN STATION

△ All the stations in the network were well cared for, with plenty of planting and decoration. This is Presteign, probably in the 1920s, with the branch train for Titley preparing to depart.

△ In 1964 there were still a number of wagons in Kington yard. A Class 1400 GWR locomotive from the 1930s simmers quietly while a leisurely shunting discussion takes place.

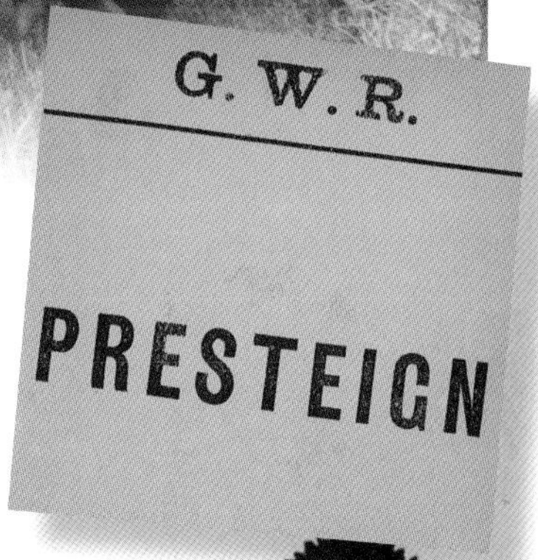

G.W.R.

PRESTEIGN

▽ By 1964 the platform was overgrown but the buildings were still in reasonable order. The pick-up goods waits to depart. The surviving station nameboard reflects uncertainty about the final letter E in Presteign.

PRESTEIGN

◁ When this photograph was taken, Tilley Junction had not seen a train for some years. The track has been lifted but, remarkably, trolleys and signs remain on the abandoned station platforms.

▽ Near New Radnor the trackbed, though overgrown, is still well defined in the hilly landscape, its route marked by the old boundary fencing. This must have been a delightful railway journey.

▷ Stanner station was one of two between Kington and New Radnor. It was little more than a halt, yet it boasted a sturdy stone building, which survives today. Despite the early closure date, this network still has a surprising amount of its original infrastructure.

△ Part of the route south of Presteign is clearly defined as a farm track through the green fields. If there was any doubt, the remains of the old sign with its rusty track support make clear the path's railway origins.

SCRAPBOOK : WALES

VICTORIAN RAILWAY BUILDERS responded to the challenges posed by the Welsh landscape by creating a network that reached many corners of the country. The first main line ran along the northern coast to Holyhead, a relatively easy journey, but those that followed, across the country and along the west coast, had to conquer more difficult terrain. Much of the development in the south of Wales was prompted by the coal industry, whose needs brought the railway into every valley. By the late 1800s the Welsh network was impressive and remarkably comprehensive. However, by the nature of the country, many lines served rural regions and catered largely for local needs, both freight and passenger.

▷ Harlech is still a much-used station on the Cambrian Coast line, set in the plain far below the town. However, long gone are the days when the railway was vital to the success of the local market. In this 1950s view cattle wagons wait in the station, while in the foreground the auctions are in full swing.

▽ At Afon Wen Junction the line south from Caernarvon met the main Cambrian Coast route, as the station sign indicates. There is a lady guard in the driver's compartment of the motor train, so this picture may date from World War I. Meanwhile, station staff deal with something difficult on the platform. This line closed in 1964, but the section east from Caernarvon to Bangor survived until 1970.

▽ By the early 1960s it was becoming apparent that much of the British Railways network faced an uncertain future, with many lines and stations scheduled for closure. This prompted the running of many specials, to allow enthusiasts the chance to visit lines that were under threat. A major player in this business was the Railway Correspondence and Travel Society (RCTS), one of whose specials visited Caernarvon on Sunday 22 August 1962. Here, the locomotive, a large LMS-built Class 3MT tank No. 40078, takes on water. In the background, a line of cattle wagons indicates the main freight traffic of the region.

▷ British Railways did much to retain and encourage traffic and to attract the tourist. One of the many ideas of this era was the Land Cruise, usually a circular tour in a train equipped with refreshments and commentary facilities, as advertised on this 1959 handbill.

NORTH WALES RADIO LAND CRUISE

SPECIALLY EQUIPPED FOR ACTUAL RADIO RECEPTION AND DESCRIPTIVE COMMENTARY ON FEATURES OF INTEREST EN ROUTE.

FOR MAP OF ROUTE PLEASE SEE OVERLEAF.

TUESDAYS and THURSDAYS
7th JULY to 23rd JULY, 1959 (inclusive)

ALSO

MONDAYS to FRIDAYS
27th JULY to 4th SEPTEMBER, 1959 (inclusive)

FARE	Time of departure	FROM	Arrival on Return
s. d.	a.m.		p.m.
	10 10	PWLLHELI	5·C25
	10 18	PENYCHAIN	5·C15
	10 30	CRICCIETH	5·C15
	10 42	PORTMADOC	5 18
13/-	10 50	PENRHYNDEUDRAETH	5 26
	10*40	TALSARNAU	5 37
FROM	11 0	HARLECH	5 42
EACH STATION	10*57	LLANBEDR & PENSARN	5 50
	11 12	DYFFRYN ARDUDWY	5 58
	11 15	TALYBONT HALT	6 6
	11 25	BARMOUTH	6 12
	11 45	PENMAENPOOL	6 17
	11 50	DOLGELLEY	7 *36
	11‡25	BALA	7 *41
	p.m.		8‡*42
	12 50	CORWEN	9 * 3

RHYL arrive 1·58 p.m.   RHYL depart 3·30 p.m.

*—Change at Barmouth.   ‡—Change at Bala Junction and Corwen.   C—Change at Afon Wen   †—Change at Bala Junction.

Children under Three years of age, Free; Three and under Fourteen years of age, Half-fare.

LIGHT MEALS AND REFRESHMENTS, MAY BE OBTAINED FROM THE CAFETERIA CAR ON THE TRAIN.

HOLIDAY RUNABOUT TICKETS ARE NOT AVAILABLE BY THIS TRAIN

For conditions of issue of these tickets, also luggage allowances, see the British Transport Commission's Regulations and Conditions of Issue of Tickets, etc.

Further information will be supplied on application to the Stations, or to Mr. O. VELTOM, District Traffic Superintendent, Oswestry (Telephone Oswestry 189, Extn. 211); Mr. W. GRIFFITHS, District Commercial Manager, Shrewsbury (Telephone Shrewsbury 3614, Extn. 65) or to Mr. E. FLAXMAN, Commercial Officer, Paddington Station, W.1.

BRITISH RAILWAYS

△ A summer scene at Towyn, on the Cambrian Coast route, in 1963: about to enter the station from a siding beyond the signal box is the local to Barmouth; on the adjacent siding a pick-up goods waits; on the platform empty milk bottles are on their way back to Machynlleth; and a family get ready to take the train.

▷ It took a long time, despite many schemes, for trains to reach Cardigan. The slow and meandering line finally opened in 1886, with nine intermediate stations, one of which was Login. Late one day in May 1962, the 4pm train from Whitland to Cardigan drifts into the station. About three months later the line was closed.

▷ Trawsfynydd, on the Bala-to-Blaenau Ffestiniog line, had – in addition to the main station – three subsidiary halts: for the power station, for the military camp and this one, Trawsfynydd Lake Halt. In the 1950s it looks insignificant and run down, but this young woman expects a train to stop.

Holiday Haunts Book Marker

Great Western Railway

◁ The GWR did much to attract traffic onto its extensive Welsh network. This, from a famous series of bookmarks, promotes the Vale of Llangollen.

▽ Trains reached Blaenau Ffestiniog from three directions. First to arrive was the narrow gauge Festiniog Railway from Porthmadog. The big companies came later, in pursuit of slate traffic: the LNWR from the north, along the Conway valley from Llandudno Junction, and the GWR from Bala in the south, along a notably wandering route. There were initially 18 intermediate stations, and trains could take 80 minutes to cover the 25 miles. Manod, where these two passengers are waiting patiently, was near the Blaenau Ffestiniog end. The line closed in 1960.

▷ Gobowen station, opened by the Chester & Shrewsbury Railway in the 1840s, is a grand structure in Italianate style, dwarfing the minor line it now serves. In the 1950s it was a busier place. Here, passengers, some in fine summer frocks, watch County Class locomotive No. 1026 'County of Salop' as it hauls a Shrewsbury-bound train into the platform.

▽ Pentir Rhiw was on the Brecon & Merthyr line south of Talyllyn Junction, part of a network mostly closed in the early 1960s. Here, in 1961 and near the end, driver and signalman prepare to exchange single-line tokens.

△ In May 1962 a local from Moat Lane Junction makes its way along the embankment south of Marteg Halt, en route to Rhayader, Builth Wells and Brecon.

E.R.O. 31985
OP.2

L. M. S.   No. 101

TRAIN STAFF TICKET

BETHESDA BRANCH

TRAIN No..............   UP
TO THE DRIVER
You are authorised, after seeing the train staff for
the Section, to proceed from
BETHESDA to BANGOR No. I,
and the Train Staff will follow.

Signature of
Date............Person in charge...........
This Ticket must be given up by the Driver
immediately on arrival, to the person in
charge of the Staff Working at the place
to which he is authorised to proceed,
to be cancelled and forwarded
to the Chief Operating
Manager.

▷ Wales was richly endowed with minimal halts on remote lines, with little for waiting passengers to do but admire the landscape. This one is Bryngwyn Halt, on the Llanfyllin branch from Llanymynech. It closed in January 1965.

STAFF

Until the 1960s hundreds of thousands of men and women were involved in the day-to-day running of Britain's railway network. A few jobs were glamorous, but most were mundane, boring, repetitive and not well paid. The successful running of the railways depended upon the strict application of structures, rules and schedules. Yet the sense of pride, commitment and dedication to the railway and to the people using it was remarkable. The thousands of photographs that survive of ordinary railway employees make this abundantly clear.

▲ This photograph was taken somewhere on the GWR network, probably in the 1930s. The two men, perhaps a porter and a signalman, pose comfortably with the small boy, who may well belong to one of them. The railway was often a family business, especially in rural areas, and it was never too soon to get the children interested.

◄ Most formal portraits of railway staff in the late Victorian and Edwardian eras were taken in the studio, usually to celebrate a promotion or some other significant event. In this case, George Pitt, an Acton photographer, has taken his equipment to the railway to take this portrait of a now anonymous driver.

▲ This unusual but carefully posed photograph shows an LNWR guard, apparently captured in the process of inspecting his train in the goods yard.

▲ Unusually, this photograph is fully captioned: 'Driver Jack Rintoul poses on J35 locomotive No. 64519 at St Leonards (Scotland), 2.5.61.' It then continues: 'Branch now closed. Loco scrapped. Driver retired.'

▶ This photograph, a dramatic image from the 1930s, shows a signalman carrying out maintenance or a running repair to a signal under his care. At the time, this would have been an everyday occurrence in the often solitary, yet highly responsible, life of a railway signalman.

▲ The rituals of maintenance were crucial elements in the safe running of the railway. Steam locomotives in particular demanded constant care and attention. Here, in Newcastle in the 1930s, a driver looks after the locomotive whose well-being is largely his responsibility.

▲ A driver in a departmental locomotive and two shunters with their poles pose in some British Railways depot in the 1950s. The setting is unremarkable, yet the image is an accurate reflection of the attitude of railway personnel of that era.

SOUTH WALES COAL TRAFFIC

FROM THE DAWN OF RAILWAYS, coal carrying was always important. However, the density of coal traffic was probably at its greatest in South Wales, with rival railway companies set up to service the many pits in the valleys. Over many decades there was plenty of coal to be carried down to the docks in Cardiff, Swansea, Newport and Barry, and small companies such as the Taff Vale and the Rhymney flourished alongside the big names, the GWR, the LNWR and the Midland. From the 1960s coal traffic diminished, and then the pit closures from the 1980s had a devastating effect, particularly in South Wales.

▷ In the 1950s the railways still carried 70 per cent of Britain's coal traffic. By the 1960s this had begun to diminish. This view, in the summer of 1964, shows the huge freight yard at Aberbeeg, with a Class 37 diesel locomotive winding its way through at the head of a long coal train. Ten years earlier the sidings would have been filled with lines of coal wagons.

△ Despite having vanished from the British Railways network in 1968, steam survived well into the 1970s in industrial locations, and notably at coal mines. In May 1974 an old saddle tank locomotive is still at work, shunting loaded wagons at Mountain Ash colliery. The main line is just visible in the left foreground.

▷ By the late 1980s things were changing fast in South Wales, as in all coal-producing areas of Britain. The massive closure programme that followed the 1984 strike tore the heart out of the traditional life of the Valleys. Yet, some collieries survived, primarily to satisfy the needs of power stations and the steel industry. Here, in 1989, two Class 37 locomotives bring a trainload of coal hoppers from the Betws mine into the Abernant Coal Preparation Plant.

◁ Still active in 1987 was Marine colliery in Ebbw Vale. Against a classic colliery background a Class 37 diesel hauls its train of wagons slowly past the mountain of coal as the excavators load them. The line on the right of the picture served the British Steel plant.

EMPTY TO HILL'S PLYMOUTH Colliery MERTHYR. G.W.R.

◁ At Abernant the driver of the Class 37 diesel pauses his coal train and leans out to take the token from the signalman. This is a timeless scene, but it is 1989 and closure threatens the future of the South Wales pits.

▽ In 1991 Tower colliery was still a major producer. Here, a heavy coal train enters the junction at Pontypridd, with the Rhondda line swinging away to the left. In the foreground the station is being rebuilt to cater for increased passenger traffic.

▽ In 1971 two elderly tank locomotives, one retired from GWR service in 1958 and the other built for industrial use by Avonside in 1914, work hard to bank a diesel-hauled coal train away from Mountain Ash, and help it on its way to the Aberaman Phurnacite Plant. Passenger services were withdrawn from this line in 1964.

EMPTY TO
CASTLE PIT
ABERCANAID. G.W.R.

△ In a scene that captures perfectly the atmosphere and history of the Valleys, a Class 37 locomotive winds its train of empties for Cwmbargoed past Bedlinog in April 1994.

SLATE & STONE

TODAY, WALES IS FAMOUS for its ever-popular, and increasing, network of passenger-carrying narrow gauge lines. It is, therefore, easy to forget that most of these lines owed their origins, and their early success, to the slate and stone industries. They were mineral lines predominantly, linking quarries to ports and harbours on the north and west coast. Despite the steady decline of this industry, some lines continued to operate commercially at least until the 1960s, but this trade has now vanished, along with its railways.

▷ The history of the Corris Railway stretches back to the 1850s. Built to link slate quarries near Aberllefenni with a quay on the river Dyfi, it began carrying passengers in 1883. In 1930 the line was acquired by the GWR, which soon abandoned passenger carrying but maintained the slate traffic, until flooding in August 1948 closed the line. In May 1948 the railway was on its last legs, but a horse was still employed in shunting duties at Aberllefenni, to the north of Corris.

▽ The most famous slate railway was the Festiniog Railway, with its dramatic line linking the vast network of slate quarries around Blaenau Ffestiniog with the harbour at Porthmadog. An early carrier of passengers, from 1865, and a pioneer tourist railway, the Festiniog nonetheless maintained its slate traffic virtually until the line closed in 1946. Restoration began in 1954, and the line's revival and subsequent success is another story. This 1934 photograph shows 'Welsh Pony', an 1867 locomotive, hauling slate wagons at Blaenau.

▷ Another famous quarry railway linked the Dinorwic quarries to Port Dinorwic, north of Caernarvon. In 1956 these were still productive, as this photograph shows. A typical locomotive is overshadowed by a landscape of slate.

▽ The Glyn Valley Tramway, built from the 1870s, ran from Chirk to quarries near Hendre. Passengers were carried from the early 1890s until closure in the 1930s. Quarry products could be transferred to the GWR main line at Chirk, as shown here in this photograph taken during the 1920s.

▽ The Penrhyn quarry network was to the south of Bangor, with a main line from Port Penrhyn to Bethesda, shown here in this 1961 photograph.

WELSH PORTS & HARBOURS

THE SOUTH WALES COAST was marked by a series of major dock complexes, most of which owe their development to the railway age. In the Victorian era the export of coal was the primary business, but by the 20th century the cargoes had became more diversified and general. This remained the pattern until the 1960s, when the trade began to diminish, leading ultimately to many docks being closed.

In West Wales the harbours were dedicated to passenger services, military activities and, more recently, to the oil trade, while in the north the slate industry was dominant, at least until the early 1900s. Not to be forgotten are the many little ports and harbours whose livelihood came from fishing and tourism.

Taff Vale Railway.
CARDIFF, T.V.
TO
PENARTH DOCK.

◁ In 1936, when this advertisement was issued, the GWR owned and operated docks at Newport, Cardiff, Port Talbot, Swansea and Barry, and the railway company benefited hugely from the still extensive import and export business that these dock complexes represented.

▽ This postcard view of Cardiff docks was sent in November 1928. The writer, a merchant seaman, says that his boat will be sailing for Galway the next day, and he points out to his wife or girlfriend the quays where they unload cement and load coal. As can be seen, everything was railway-connected.

▷ ▽ Even the smallest harbours were often linked to the railway network, to facilitate the handling of coastal trade and passenger traffic. These Edwardian cards show the pier and quay at Aberdovey (right) and the pier at Barry docks (below), which was used primarily for passenger services. A train has just arrived at Barry, and the passengers are walking towards the quay where a paddle steamer waits, bound perhaps for North Devon or the resorts of West Wales. Loaded coal wagons sit in an adjacent siding.

50844. ABERDOVEY. VIEW FROM PIER.

BARRY PIER.

GREAT WESTERN RAILWAY.
(1325)
W 34 10,000/1/13.
URGENT
From Alexandra Dock Junction, NEWPORT, Mon.
To
Route via
Wagon No.
Train   Sheet No.
Consignee   Date   191
Charges to pay £

▽ In the early 1960s many docks were still busy with railway activity. Here, in August 1962, a former GWR tank locomotive, No. 6658, hauls a mixed freight along the dockside at Barry, en route for Cardiff.

▷ An iron boundary post survives from the Alexandra (Newport & South Wales) Docks & Railway Company, whose network opened in 1875.

NARROW GAUGE RAILWAYS : WALES

WALES IS FAMOUS as the land of little trains, with
a great variety of lines dedicated to tourism. However,
from the 1830s, when the first iron-railed quarry lines
opened, until about 1900, Welsh narrow gauge existed
primarily for the transport of slate from quarry to
harbour or to standard gauge railhead. Initially lines
were horse-operated, but steam was used from 1848.
It was only as the slate industry declined that passenger
carrying became important and, as this was coincidental
with the rise of tourism, many lines – including Talyllyn
and Festiniog – gained a fresh lease of life. At the same
time, new railways opened aimed at the tourist market.

▽ This evocative and carefully posed photograph shows a Festiniog
Railway train at Tan-y-Bwlch, perhaps in the 1890s. Opened in 1836
to link quarries at Blaenau Ffestiniog to Porthmadog, the railway
developed its distinctive range of steam locomotives from the 1860s.
From the 1880s the Festiniog sought to replace declining slate traffic
with passenger services aimed at tourists, marketing itself as The Toy
Railway. Closed in 1946 and reopened in 1955, the railway is now
a premier tourist line.

△ Opened in 1859 to serve slate quarries in the Aberllefenni and Corris
regions above Machynlleth, the Corris Railway carried passengers from
1883 and indeed was a pioneer in the development of railway tourism
in Wales. This shows one of the original 1878 Falcon locomotives hard
at work, perhaps in the early 1900s. The line closed in 1948.

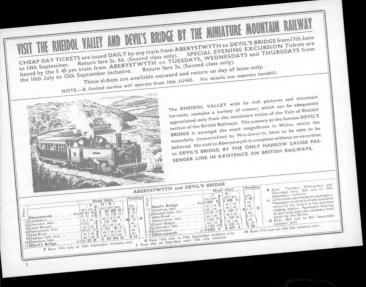

△ One of a pair of locomotives built by the GWR for the Vale of Rheidol in 1923, 'Owain Glyndwr' is seen here in the 1970s, during the period of British Rail operation. Marketed as the last BR steam service, the railway passed to private ownership in 1988.

△ The Vale of Rheidol railway, opened in 1902 primarily as a passenger line with some freight interests, became an important part of the tourist infrastructure in the Aberystwyth region. It enjoyed a chequered career, being owned by the GWR and British Railways. In the 1950s BR tried hard to promote the line, as this brochure indicates.

△ Another great name in the history of Welsh narrow gauge railways is the Talyllyn, famous today as the first to be saved and reopened by enthusiasts. It started in 1866 as a slate line, linking quarries with Tywyn harbour and offering limited passenger services. By the 1930s, when this photograph was taken, it was dedicated to tourism.

△ Taken at Abergynolwyn in August 1954, in the exciting days of pioneering preservation by railway enthusiasts, this shows the locomotive 'Douglas', built by Barclay in 1918 and acquired by the Talyllyn in 1953.

▷ The Glyn Valley Tramway, opened in 1873, was built to serve slate quarries west of Chirk but from an early date also carried passengers, as this Edwardian card of Glynceiriog shows. The line closed in 1935.

MINIATURE RAILWAYS : WALES

IN A COUNTRY famous for narrow gauge railways, it is easy to forget that miniature lines have also been important. First on any list is the Fairbourne, whose history goes back to 1890 when, built to encourage the development of Fairbourne as a resort, it opened as a horse-drawn tramway linked to a ferry to Barmouth. Another line with a significant history opened at Rhyl in 1911. Inevitably most of the dozen or so lines that have operated in Wales were sited in popular coastal resorts, with the majority in the north of the country.

"Belle of New York" Model Engine arrives at Gwrych Castle Station, Abergele, 11887

Opening of the Rhyl Miniature Railway, May 4th, 1911.
First Train leaving the Station.

△ A short line was opened in the late 1940s in the grounds of Gwrych Castle, an early 19th-century folly near the north coast resort of Abergele. This 1950s image shows the line's particular character, and an American-style locomotive.

◁ This card records the opening of Rhyl's famous 15in gauge railway in May 1911. It was an important, pioneering line, and its lakeside circuit was planned by Henry Greenly, using Bassett-Lowke locomotives.

△ This 1960s card shows a busy day on the Colwyn Bay railway, which ran for about 500 yards along the seafront. Opened in the early 1950s, it closed in about 1988. At that time, 'Prince Charles', shown here, was the railway's only locomotive.

▽ In a classic miniature railway scene, a young enthusiast takes a break from the beach to examine this grand locomotive on a miniature Welsh line.

△ Porthcawl's 15in gauge line opened in 1932, between Salt Lake and Coney Beach, and closed in 1986. On this postcard we see 'Coney Queen', a petrol-driven, steam-outline locomotive.

◁ This colourful image shows Prestatyn's miniature railway in the 1970s, with one of its BR diesel-style locomotives. The line closed in the early 1980s.

△ The Fairbourne Railway has enjoyed a long and eventful history, with several changes of gauge and ownership. It is seen here during the 1950s.

MODEL TRAIN SETS

SERIOUS RAILWAY MODELLING, as opposed to toy trains, emerged in the late 1800s, notably in Germany, then the home of lithographed tinplate. An increasing concern for accuracy and detail resulted in complete layouts, with many vehicle variants and numerous accessories. The father of model railways in Britain was WJ Bassett-Lowke, who commissioned Bing, in Germany, to manufacture British-style locomotives and rolling stock and later developed his own business. Other names joined in, notably Bonds, Leeds Model Co and, most important, Frank Hornby. Hornby began with 0 gauge clockwork toy trains and in the 1930s introduced the extensive 00 gauge electric tabletop range that still carries his name. Since the 1950s, 00 and the smaller N gauge have dominated an international market, prompting domestic, club and exhibition railway modelling across the world.

▲ The permanent large-scale, 0 gauge layout featured on this postcard was built at New Romney station in Kent to attract visitors to the Romney, Hythe & Dymchurch Railway, one of Britain's premier miniature lines.

MODEL TRAINS WORKING ON THE BRITISH RAILWAYS EXHIBIT.
THIS IS GUAGE "O" AND THE MODEL TRAINS WERE SPECIALLY MADE FOR THE BRITISH RAILWAYS EXHIBIT AT GLASGOW AND ARE ALL ELECTRICALLY DRIVEN AND OPERATED.
MODELS BY BASSETT-LOWKE LTD., OF NORTHAMPTON, LONDON & MANCHESTER.

L.M.S. CORONATION SCOT DRAWN BY L.M.S. PACIFIC LOCOMOTIVE "CORONATION."

THE L.N.E.R. CORONATION TRAIN DRAWN BY PACIFIC TYPE LOCOMOTIVE "DOMINION OF CANADA."

THE G.W.R. CORNISH RIVIERA DRAWN BY LOCOMOTIVE "KING GEORGE V."

THE SOUTHERN ELECTRIC TRAIN DRAWN BY THE ELECTRIC BOGIE

▲ From 1948 British Railways developed a large model railway layout, 40ft long, with 700ft of track. This was transported around the country and demonstrated for promotional purposes.

▲ This postcard shows the up-to-date models made by Bassett-Lowke for the British Railways exhibit at the Glasgow International Exhibition in 1938, featuring trains from the Big Four.

BRITISH RAILWAYS TRAIN SETS

▶ For the dedicated modeller, manufacturers' catalogues could be augmented by those from the numerous specialist suppliers of rolling stock, accessories and landscape features. There has also long been a range of literature, including magazines, as well as regional clubs, devoted to those who want to build their own models.

MAINLINE RAILWAYS

Tri-ang RAILWAYS

'OO' Scale Model Catalogue XXII

Hornby Railways

▲▲▶ Annual catalogues produced from the 1930s by names such as Bassett-Lowke and Hornby, and later by Tri-ang, Trix, Peco, Wrenn, Mainline and others, give an insight into an ever-expanding business and often have a wonderful period quality.

Edward Beal's
RAILWAY MODELLING SERIES

Book Six
WAGONS
AND
COACHES

4/6

Published by
Modelcraft
77, GROSVENOR RD., LONDON S.W.1.

PECO Nº 1
MODEL RAILWAY PRODUCTS

R.687 SILVER JUBILEE PULLMAN SET

SILVER JUBILEE SET

BASSETT-LOWKE
GAUGE 'O' SCALE MODEL RAILWAYS

HORNBY
DUBLO
ELECTRIC TRAINS
MADE AND GUARANTEED BY MECCANO LTD

A Complete Railway on a Table

CENTRAL
ENGLAND

THE MARLOW BRANCH

IN 1854 THE WYCOMBE RAILWAY opened its line from High Wycombe to Maidenhead. This was a broad gauge line, one of a number planned for the High Wycombe area. IK Brunel was its engineer. Included on its route was a station called Marlow Road, later Bourne End, but this was not enough for local businessmen, who campaigned for a branch line from here to Marlow itself. This, the grandly named Great Marlow Railway, was completed in 1873. From the start, this short branch was operated by an 1868 tank locomotive, No. 522. Remaining in service until 1935, it was known as the 'Marlow Donkey', a name that has been associated with the branch ever since. In 1970 the line from High Wycombe to Bourne End closed, thus making the entire route from Maidenhead to Marlow a modern branch line.

G. W. R.
———————
Marlow

▽ Steam survived on the Marlow branch until the early 1960s. Here, in an unusual driver's view taken during June 1962, former GWR tank locomotive No. 1445 approaches the terminus at Marlow. As the branch was under 3 miles long, it was usually operated by one train. At this time there were 19 trains a day each way.

◁ By the late 1970s, when this photograph was taken, the line from Bourne End to High Wycombe had gone. Therefore Bourne End had become in effect a terminus, requiring trains on the branch to reverse. Here, DMUs bound for Marlow and Maidenhead meet at Bourne End.

△ On a summer's evening in 1978 the 19.39 DMU service from Marlow approaches Cookham station.

▷ This card, which was in fact posted from Worcester in 1908, shows Marlow from the Thames, a view then – as now – dominated by the church and the suspension bridge, just visible in the distance. At this point Marlow was a quiet but popular Thames-side resort, though clearly not a rival for Henley or Maidenhead.

Great Marlow.

△ From its opening in 1873 until the end of steam in the summer of 1962, the Marlow branch was usually operated by a single train. Here, on a quiet day in the late 1950s the 'Marlow Donkey' of that era waits in the platform at Marlow in the care of former GWR tank locomotive No. 1445, while some essential servicing and cleaning is carried out.

▷ Despite the deserted nature of this 1953 view, Marlow station was at times busy. It was popular with commuters and shoppers and, during the season, there were visitors wanting to enjoy the pleasures of the Thames. Here, engine shed, signal box, signal and station sign give it a typical GWR branchline atmosphere.

△ The centenary of the Marlow branch was marked in July 1973 by a steam special. Here, hauled by preserved GWR Modified Hall Class No. 6998 'Burton Agnes Hall', the long train climbs away from Bourne End, with lots of heads at the windows enjoying the spectacle.

▷ In its heyday, Marlow was a typical branchline terminus, with a goods yard, signal box and engine shed. Today, modern trains creep into a single platform in a remote part of the town, with the most basic of station buildings. However, there is at least a flowerbed, hinting at better things in the past. And perhaps modern travellers should be grateful that trains still run to Marlow, a rare branchline survivor.

BLETCHLEY TO BEDFORD

PLANS TO BUILD A RAILWAY to Bedford go back to the 1830s, but nothing happened until the next decade when, encouraged by George Stephenson, the Bedford Railway was formed to build a branch from Bletchley. It was constructed by the London & Birmingham Railway and opened in 1846, but was soon absorbed into the L&NWR. Initially isolated, Bedford quickly became an important railway centre,

and the former Bletchley-to-Bedford branch became part of the cross-country route linking Oxford and Cambridge. The original branch line's early date is underlined in a series of distinctive timber-framed stations, built at the behest of the Duke of Bedford where the line ran through his Woburn estate. Their survival gives a memorial quality to one of the more remote routes in the modern network.

◁ From 1838 Bletchley was an important station on the route of the London & Birmingham Railway. It was for a short time a terminus, owing to delays in the completion of Kilsby tunnel. In this 1950s view the station seems remarkably quiet, with plenty of bicycles and platform clutter but very few people.

▷ Apart from the four timber-framed stations, the buildings on the Bletchley line were rather unremarkable. The crossing houses were built in the popular Gothic style of the 1840s, as seen here at Bow Brickhill in the 1950s, with characteristically low platform, small signal box and basic waiting room.

◁ This rural view of Woburn Sands station was published in the Edwardian era and captures the atmosphere of the line. This was one of the four timber-framed stations reflecting the taste of the Duke of Bedford, the others being Fenny Stratford, Ridgmont and Millbrook.

▽ Woburn Abbey was always a popular destination for excursions, as this 1964 handbill indicates. However, the bus connection was from Flitwick, on the main line, and not from Woburn Sands, which was actually closer.

The Station, Woburn Sands

▽ By the 1990s the line had seen better days. The track is overgrown and a single-car DMU, or 'Bubble Car', seen here leaving Stewartby, was sufficient for the few passengers using it. Semaphore signals are still in use. The tall chimneys recall the vast amount of traffic generated in early times by the region's brickworks.

△ The original terminus station was Bedford St John's, seen here perhaps in the 1920s. It is busy with freight traffic, mostly open plank wagons for the brick industry, but only one passenger waits on the platform.

▽ This photograph of a modern train stopping at Millbrook station shows the improvements made to the line since 2000. The original 1846 timber-framed station building survives as a private house.

△ This 1911 card of Fenny Stratford shows the main street of one of the larger towns along the route. The message on the back is predictable: 'Arrived quite safe. Weather very grand.'

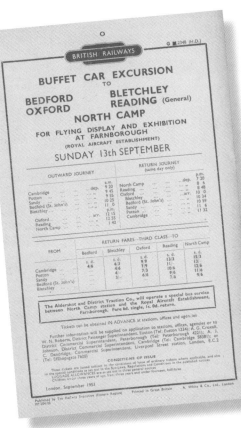

BEDFORD, EMBANKMENT FROM TOWN BRIDGE   81452

△ Bedford has a number of attractions for visitors, chief among them being its situation on the river Great Ouse, shown to advantage on this 1930s card. It is also the birthplace of John Bunyan, who famously began writing *The Pilgrim's Progress* while in Bedford gaol.

△ This 1953 handbill promotes a buffet car excursion from Cambridge and other stations to the Farnborough Air Show. The route from Cambridge to Oxford, now lost, included the Bletchley-to-Bedford line.

THE SPILSBY BRANCH

A BRANCH LINE TO SPILSBY from Firsby on the long-established East Lincolnshire Railway's Grimsby-to-Boston line was authorized in June 1865. It was a largely local enterprise, so construction was slow, and the 4-mile Spilsby & Firsby Railway did not open until May 1868. It was worked by the Great Northern, which eventually took it over, in 1891. In 1923 it became part of the LNER, and the weekday service of six trains each way continued until 10 September 1939, when passenger trains were stopped as a wartime economy measure. They were never resumed, but freight lasted until December 1958. Today, buildings survive to define the route but, in an open agricultural landscape, much else has vanished.

◁ This card of Spilsby station was posted in 1911, with a romantic message on the back for Alice Lake of King's Lynn from 'her ever loving friend', who sends her six kisses.

Station and Boston Road

SPILSBY

▷ Little of the trackbed remains in the flat landscape, but the sites of level crossings can be identified, often marked by distinctive crossing-keepers' cottages, now private houses. Typical is this example at Mill Lane, where there is a cottage, a crossing gate (perhaps not the original one, but attached to the old concrete post), and the remains of a ganger's hut.

▽ In May 1954 a famous Lincolnshire railtour included the Spilsby branch. This shows the train's arrival at Spilsby, hauled by J6 Class No. 64199. Nothing remains of the station today, and the site is covered by a supermarket.

HALTON HOLGATE, SPILSBY

△ ▷ There was only one intermediate station, Halton Holgate, a small farming village. Today, apart from the cars, it still looks much as it did in this 1920s postcard. There is still a Station Road, albeit with its nameplate half-hidden in vegetation.

◁ Halton Holgate station survives as a private house and, despite the addition of a conservatory, can easily be identified from the adjacent road bridge. The goods shed also remains, hidden in the depths of the garden.

▽ Taken from the same bridge in the 1950s, when the branch was open for freight traffic, this photograph shows Halton Holgate station still virtually complete. It was a substantial building for a small village, with a coal yard and a large goods shed, all set in what was then more open countryside.

◁ The branch crossed the main road to meet the main line. The crossing cottage survives, and nearby, just visible in the overgrowth, is the platform edge.

▽ Firsby, opened in 1848 by the East Lincolnshire Railway, was a grand station, and the junction for branches to Spilsby and Skegness. The main line to Grimsby closed in 1970, and Firsby station was subsequently demolished – except for this fragment.

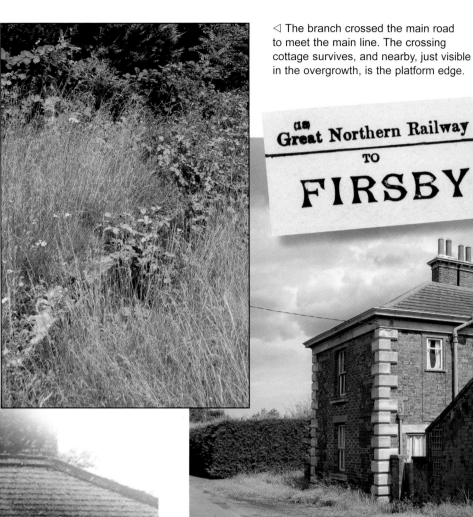

(the) **Great Northern Railway**

TO

FIRSBY

△ This photograph shows Firsby's station around the time of its closure in 1970. The central section of the building, with its classical portico, was flanked by matching wings. The wing nearest the camera is seen in the more recent picture above.

THE WOODSTOCK BRANCH

THERE WERE MANY CASES in Victorian Britain of railways being sponsored by wealthy landowners for their own purposes. Less familiar than some is the Woodstock Railway, financed by the Duke of Marlborough to service Blenheim Palace and opened in May 1890. A little over 2 miles long, the branch left the GWR's main line near Kidlington, north of Oxford. The GWR was soon involved in the running of the railway and took control of it in 1897. There

was one intermediate halt between Kidlington and Blenheim & Woodstock, at Shipton-on-Cherwell. The line's unremarkable route was a mix of low embankments and cuttings across the fields, and it continued to operate until 1954. In 1947 there were eight trains a day each way, on weekdays only. Today, little remains to be seen. Inaccessible embankments and infilled cuttings mark the route, one being a footpath and nature reserve.

Blenheim Palace : S. Front

△ The Duke of Marlborough's magnificent 17th-century palace at Blenheim was the main reason for the building of the Woodstock branch. This card, showing the south front, was posted in Oxford on 6 August 1914. At that point World War I was two days old, and the writer, presumably a regular soldier, says that he is being sent to Swindon in order to 'guard the railways'.

G.W.R.
Blenheim AND Woodstock

◁ The single-track branch was token-operated from Kidlington Junction. This 1950s photograph shows the token being handed over by the Kidlington signalman.

△ The line skirted the little canalside village of Shipton-on-Cherwell. Today, although infilling has occurred, the route can just about be identified. This sign is a convenient reminder of the former branch line.

◁ A famous locomotive long associated with the branch was GWR 517 Class tank No. 1473, suitably named 'Fair Rosamund'. This 1930 photograph shows the engine and its single carriage waiting for passengers at Blenheim & Woodstock.

△ Blenheim & Woodstock station was set well to the east of Woodstock town centre. In this 1950s photograph, taken perhaps around the time of the line's closure, the Vauxhall car adds a nice period touch. Subsequent rebuilding has largely hidden the station site.

▽ The line's main engineering feature was the long embankment that carried it over the A423 Banbury road. Today, the overgrown bridge abutments survive, but the embankment itself is a secret and hidden world in which sections of trackbed can still be identified.

CLEOBURY MORTIMER & DITTON PRIORS

THE CLEOBURY MORTIMER & DITTON PRIORS RAILWAY was a typical product of the Light Railway Act of 1894. It was an essentially local enterprise serving a remote area, and it took seven years to build the 12-mile line, which finally opened in 1908. A branch serving one of the Clee Hill quarries generated some freight traffic, but the railway was never busy and at times there were only two trains a day. Despite this, it managed to retain its independence and was not absorbed into the GWR until 1922. Passenger services ended in 1938, but traffic was maintained by an armaments depot. During World War II it was in effect a military railway, and this connection was maintained when the Admiralty took control in 1957 and operated the line until final closure in 1965.

▷ Cleobury Mortimer is an attractive market town and the site of a massive 12th-century fortress. This Edwardian card sets the scene, showing the dominant church spire.

▽ The Ditton Priors Railway started at Cleobury Mortimer, a station on the GWR line from Woofferton to Bewdley. Here, on a May afternoon in 1955, an old GWR Class 2301 locomotive, No. 2516, pauses at the station. This survives as a private house, and the locomotive has been preserved.

▷ The railway was always a minimal line, with limited facilities. This is the terminus at Ditton Priors, perhaps in the 1920s. There were nine intermediate stations, most of which were little more than halts serving isolated rural communities. Even Ditton Priors was in effect a halt, and for a time was named accordingly.

▽ Passenger services ceased in 1938, but the line was visited by enthusiasts' specials from time to time during its period of military occupation. This shows one such visit to Ditton Priors in 1955, with a long train in the care of an ancient GWR Class 2021 pannier tank locomotive, No. 2144, complete with spark-arresting chimney fitted to protect the volatile Admiralty cargoes it usually hauled.

◁ There was never much at Cleobury North Crossing station, and what little there was had largely disappeared by 1964, when this photograph was taken. A few months later the Admiralty, owners since 1957, closed the line.

GWR SPECIAL NOTICE

DISCONTINUANCE OF

PASSENGER TRAIN SERVICE

BETWEEN

CLEOBURY MORTIMER

AND

DITTON PRIORS

The Great Western Railway give notice that on and from MONDAY, SEPTEMBER 26th, 1938, the Passenger Train service on the above Line will be withdrawn and the following trains cancelled :—

9.30 a.m. Cleobury Mortimer to Ditton Priors.
2.54 p.m. (Wednesdays only) Cleobury Mortimer to Ditton Priors.
5.30 p.m. Cleobury Mortimer to Ditton Priors.
11.15 a.m. Ditton Priors to Cleobury Mortimer.
3.50 p.m. (Wednesdays only) Upton Priors to Cleobury Mortimer.
6.30 p.m. Ditton Priors to Cleobury Mortimer.

The Platform at the undermentioned places will be closed to Passengers :—

CLEOBURY TOWN HALT   ASTON BOTTERELL SIDING
DETTON FORD SIDING   BURWARTON HALT
PRESCOTT SIDING   CLEOBURY NORTH CROSSING
STOTTESDON HALT   DITTON PRIORS HALT

The Company will continue to run one Goods train in each direction over the Line on week-days only, and to afford facilities for the conveyance of Parcels traffic, Minerals, Livestock and General Merchandise to and from the above-mentioned places.

Particulars of the arrangements may be obtained on application to the Station Master, Cleobury Mortimer; Mr. E. Potter, Divisional Superintendent, Worcester (Shrub Hill Station) (Telephone 1580), or Mr. J. A. Warren-King, District Goods Manager, Worcester (Shrub Hill Station) (Telephone 1580).

PADDINGTON STATION,   JAMES MILNE,
July, 1938.   General Manager.

Printed in Great Britain by WYMAN & SONS LTD., London, Reading and Fakenham.—522.

▽ As a cheaply built light railway, the Ditton Priors line made little impact on the landscape, and after closure much of the route disappeared. However, sections can be traced, such as this low embankment across the fields near Stottesdon.

▷ The GWR withdrew passenger services in September 1938, as this handbill indicates. At that point there were two trains a day each way, with an extra service on Wednesday, market day.

△ The stations were all minimal structures yet, remarkably, some can still be traced. Here, in a wooded field, lie the remains of Burwarton station platform, with a low depression marking the former trackbed.

▷ To the untrained eye, this is just a muddy farm track. In fact, it is the route of the railway near Stottesdon. It is hard to believe that trains ran here 50 years ago.

SCRAPBOOK : CENTRAL ENGLAND

MOST RAILWAY MAPS of Central England produced in the first half of the 20th century are dominated by the great main lines running northwards from London, supported by a dense network of interconnecting cross-country routes. What these tend to overshadow is the wealth of minor and branch lines that until the 1960s were a major feature of this region. Almost extinct in Central England today, they are well represented in the pages that follow. Some lines were remote and rural, while others served urban centres until driven out of existence by cars and buses.

▽ The habit of decorating trains for special occasions, both national and local, was common in late Victorian Britain. This resplendent GNR locomotive stands ready in Hitchin yard to haul the train for the Engineers' Department Free Trip – probably part of Queen Victoria's Golden Jubilee celebrations in 1887.

▷ A classic roadside line, the Wantage Tramway opened in 1875. Initially horse-drawn, it later featured the type of tram engine shown here. Passenger carrying ended in 1925, but the passenger vehicles lingered on a while, abandoned in a siding.

△ Though planned by the Swindon & Highworth Railway, this short branch was completed by the GWR, who opened it in 1883. After an uneventful life, it closed to passengers in 1953 but remained open for freight for a short time. This shows a visit to Highworth by an enthusiasts' special in March 1962.

◁ In October 1963 a former LMS Ivatt tank locomotive, No. 41222, propels its train into Great Linford station, on the short branch from Wolverton to Newport Pagnell, with its smoke drifting towards the washing line beyond the station. Less than a year later, the line was closed.

△ Two small railway companies planned branch lines to Watlington, but only the Watlington & Princes Risborough Railway completed the route, opening in 1872. The GWR soon took over, and it then survived until 1957. This is Watlington station, two days before closure.

△ Although initially a pioneer London Underground railway, the Metropolitan was ambitious, and its tentacles spread far beyond the city it served. The outer limit it reached was Verney Junction, on the Oxford-to-Bedford line.

▽ ▷ In the early 1960s the pace of closures began to accelerate. Those living on the Cheltenham-to-Kingham line who went on the Cruft's excursion in February 1962 would find their railway had gone by October the same year

BRITISH TRANSPORT COMMISSION

BRITISH RAILWAYS
(Western Region)

——

WITHDRAWAL OF PASSENGER TRAIN SERVICES BETWEEN CHELTENHAM SPA ST. JAMES' & KINGHAM

PRINTED BY JOSEPH WONES LTD., WEST BROMWICH.

WESTERN REGION

CRUFT'S DOG SHOW

DAY EXCURSION BOOKINGS
TO
LONDON
(PADDINGTON)
ON
FRIDAY, 9th FEBRUARY

△ The station staff and the crew of the GWR Class 1400 tank locomotive No. 1499 pose for the camera at Marlborough's Great Western station in May 1929. Notable are the platform signal box and the magnificent lamp. At that point Marlborough had two stations, but now it has none.

△ Malvern had a choice of interesting stations, with a couple designed by the famous local architect EW Elmslie. Two were called Malvern Wells. This is the GWR one, set to the south of the junction that led to Great Malvern station, Elmslie's masterpiece. It is the long, hard winter of 1963, and the snow still lies thickly as Class 2800 No. 3859 starts its train from the platform.

△ The narrow gauge Snailbeach Railway opened in 1877 to serve lead mines near Shrewsbury. Later, Colonel Stephens took over, and it carried granite, staggering on under various ownerships until 1959. Here, in 1989, some of the track is still visible.

◁ The exploration of closed railways has long been a popular pastime and the use of the chalked slate to identify stations is well known. This is Symonds Yat, on the line from Monmouth Troy to Ross-on-Wye, closed in January 1959.

◁ After a long gestation the Cheadle Railway opened its short branch from Cheadle to Creswell, on the Stoke-to-Uttoxeter line, in 1901. Tean, formerly Totmonslow, was the only intermediate station. By 1961 it had become a dumping ground for disused vehicles. Two years later the branch closed.

▽ This shows a Manchester train near Hanley, on the Potteries loop line, in 1963. Shelton steel works is in the background. Today, parts of the loop line are a walkway and the steel works is long gone, along with everything in the picture.

▷ The Potteries loop line from Etruria to Kidsgrove connected some of the major Stoke-on-Trent towns, including Hanley, Burslem and Tunstall. By 1960, this once-popular route had seen better days. An early DMU pauses at Kidsgrove Liverpool Road, the most northerly station on the loop, on its way to Congleton.

△ The London & Birmingham Railway established its workshops at Wolverton in 1838. Later it became the main carriage works for the LNWR and by the early 20th century it was a vast complex, including the famous Royal Train Shed of 1889. The main line north from Euston is on the right.

◁ Several early Victorian railway architects favoured the Tudor style. Typical is Rearsby, on the line from Leicester to Melton Mowbray, which was opened in 1846 by the Syston & Peterborough Railway. It survives, but it ceased to be a station in 1951.

△ This colourful Edwardian card shows Uppingham station, at the end of the short branch from Seaton, on the Stamford-to-Market Harborough line. As the postcard indicates, it was a long way from the town it served and was rarely busy, ultimately closing in the summer of 1960.

HOSPITAL RAILWAYS

About a dozen hospitals, convalescent homes and asylums in various parts of Britain were served by private stations, usually on short branches from nearby lines. Some of the hospitals were military establishments. The stations ranged from substantial structures to temporary wooden platforms, but what they had in common was the fact they did not appear in timetables, although tickets to them were sometimes issued. There were also at least three cemetery stations, two of which, the Kings Cross Funeral station serving Maiden Lane Cemetery and the Colney Hatch Cemetery branch from New Southgate, were very short-lived, in use from about 1861 to 1873.

▼ The Royal Victoria Hospital at Netley, in Hampshire, was opened in the aftermath of the Crimean war. With over 1,000 beds, it was the largest military hospital in Britain. At first, patients were delivered by ship, but in 1900 a hospital station was opened on a spur from Netley station, on the Southampton-to-Fareham line. This photograph shows the hospital station during World War I, when Netley looked after 50,000 patients. All the buildings at Netley, except the chapel, were demolished in 1966, and the site is now the Royal Victoria Country Park.

HOSPITAL STATION. NETLEY.

► Cheddleton Asylum was opened in the 1890s for patients from the Potteries area. It was served by an electric tramway, which opened in 1899 from a special platform at Leekbrook Junction station, on the Churnet Valley line. The tramway closed in the 1950s, but Leekbrook is now part of a preserved line.

Hellingly Station. 687.

▲ ◄ The Silloth Convalescent Home was opened in 1862 to offer patients from Carlisle Infirmary the chance to enjoy the 'salubrious air'. Later, a basic platform was built to serve the home. The platform and the railway, shown above in about 1910 and to the left in 1929, have gone, but the home remains.

▲ Hellingly Asylum, designed by GT Hine, was opened in 1903 near Hailsham, Sussex, complete with isolation hospital and children's unit. It was served by a short, electrically operated branch from Hellingly station, seen on the left in the postcard. Passenger services ceased in 1931 but the line remained open for goods until 1959.

▲ Whittingham Asylum was built near Preston in 1869 to the designs of Henry Littler. It was a massive enterprise, holding 1,000 male and 1,000 female patients, and including an isolation hospital and church. From 1889 to 1959 a branch from Grimsargh carried staff, visitors and coal for heating.

► The London Necropolis Company opened its cemetery at Brookwood, near Woking, in 1854, served by special trains from Waterloo until 1941. There were two stations, South for C of E, North for Catholics and others.

MINERAL TRAFFIC

AFTER COAL, THE MOST IMPORTANT railway traffic has always been minerals, particularly from iron ore and stone quarries. From the early days local lines were built directly from quarry to iron foundry, but as the network expanded, so did long-distance mineral traffic, for example from Northamptonshire to South Wales or Northeast England. Central England has always been renowned for its stone, so Oxfordshire, Northamptonshire, Leicestershire and Derbyshire have long been known for their quarry lines.

◁ Until the 1980s it was usual for major quarries, coal mines and iron and steel works to be railway-connected, for the train has always been, and always will be, the most efficient carrier of bulk products. Industrial decline in the late 20th century brought about significant changes and closures, and scenes like this became increasingly common. By 1980 British Steel's plant at Newark, in Nottinghamshire, was derelict, together with this old 1937 Hudswell Clarke industrial locomotive.

▽ Mines in the Tutbury area of Staffordshire have produced alabaster, or gypsum, since the Middle Ages. The main mine, at Fauld, used a railway to transport the alabaster blocks to a nearby mill, where they were crushed and used in the making of plaster. In 1966, when this photograph was taken, the mine was part of British Gypsum, which still operates it today.

LIMESTONE
TO
Melting Shop

H.O. 1889

▽ The Clee Hills in Shropshire were a well-known source of iron, copper and limestone. In 1864 the Ludlow & Clee Hill Railway opened its 6-mile line to serve the stone quarries, and from 1893 it was owned jointly by the GWR and the LNWR. There was also a narrow gauge inclined plane linking the Titterstone quarry to the railway. This photograph, perhaps taken in the 1950s, shows the spectacular setting and, in the foreground, remains of the narrow gauge network.

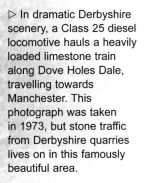

◁ Set up in 1917 to work quarries near Wroxton, west of Banbury, Oxfordshire Ironstone became one of the major iron ore producers in the Midlands. In 1965, when this photograph was taken, output had reached 40,000 tons per week. Two years later, the business went into liquidation, though some output was maintained until 1978. Little remains to be seen today of the extensive railway network, built originally by German POWs.

▷ In dramatic Derbyshire scenery, a Class 25 diesel locomotive hauls a heavily loaded limestone train along Dove Holes Dale, travelling towards Manchester. This photograph was taken in 1973, but stone traffic from Derbyshire quarries lives on in this famously beautiful area.

SOME OF ENGLAND'S earliest tramways and narrow gauge railways were built in the centre of the country to serve quarries, coal mines, clay pits and iron foundries. One of the first was the Peak Forest Tramway, opened about 1800, but other early lines include the Stratford & Moreton, the Severn & Wye and the Cauldon Low. Later came the passenger-carrying lines, mostly inspired by the expansion of travel and tourism in the first decades of the 20th century, although the transport of minerals and other freight remained important. Typical of these later lines were the two featured here.

TERMINUS OF ASHOVER LIGHT RAILWAY AT THE BUTTS ASHOVER

▽ Mineral traffic inspired the Ashover Light Railway, but by the time the 7-mile line was opened from Clay Cross to Ashover in 1925, it also carried passengers, most of them tourists drawn to explore the Derbyshire hills and dales. The railway was planned by the famous Colonel Stephens, and it bore his stamp in its construction and management. Its connection with the LMS main line was at Clay Cross & Egstow, whose rather basic station is shown here, perhaps in the late 1930s. The photograph also shows one of the original coaches, some of which were bought from the 1924 Wembley Exhibition's railway.

△ Ashover Butts was the end of the line. Its attractive setting and proximity to the Derbyshire landscape was a bonus for tourists, but it also served a local quarry that supplied rail ballast to the LMS. This helped to keep the Ashover Light Railway in business until 1950, when the loss of this regular traffic closed the line.

△ The most famous tourist line in Central England was the Leek & Manifold Valley Light Railway, whose scenic route made it popular from the day it opened in June 1904. The northern terminus was Hulme End, seen here in the 1930s.

▷ Being dependent largely upon tourist traffic, the railway promoted itself in various ways. Typical were postcards depicting the scenic qualities of the route. This 1908 example shows the landscape near Waterhouses, the line's starting point.

Manifold Railway Waterhouses.

△ This card shows Ecton station, built in the simple style associated with the Leek & Manifold. It was a stopping point for remote villages and farms set in the spectacular landscape that made the line so popular with trippers from nearby industrial towns.

▷ Although short-lived – it was closed by the LMS in 1934 – the Leek & Manifold was a distinctive and proud railway, particularly at first, when owned by the North Staffordshire Railway. Its locomotives and carriages had an exotic, Indian quality unlike any other narrow gauge line in Britain.

TRADITIONALLY, MINIATURE RAILWAYS are associated with seaside resorts, yet some of the earliest were built in the heart of England. The pioneer was Sir Arthur Heywood, who promoted the 15in gauge on a line built at his house, Duffield Bank, near Derby. The Duke of Westminster followed his lead with the Eaton Hall line in 1896, and CW Bartholomew installed an estate railway at Blakesley Hall in 1903. These were essentially private lines, but an early public railway was opened at Sutton Coldfield in 1907.

WOODLANDS RAILWAY, LOVELY LILLESHALL

△ In 1927 Herbert Ford bought Lilleshall Hall, in Staffordshire, and turned it into an amusement park. The miniature railway opened in 1930 and was operated by Bill Jeggo. When it closed in 1939, its locomotives were moved to the railway at Trentham.

KETTERING. WICKSTEED PARK. LAKE AND MINIATURE RAILWAY

◁ The Wicksteed Park Railway was opened in 1931, a 2ft gauge line around the lake in a popular park near Kettering, Northamptonshire. This 1950s card shows the diesel-powered steam outline locomotive.

▽ Trentham Gardens, to the south of Stoke-on-Trent and formerly the estate of the Dukes of Sutherland, has been a favourite with visitors since the Victorian era. A 2ft gauge miniature railway opened in 1935, with petrol-powered steam outline locomotives. Its popularity is apparent in this 1950s card.

WAY OUT ONLY

Sutton Coldfield's first line was opened in 1907 and featured the famous Bassett-Lowke engine 'Mighty Atom'. In 1937, the date of this card, the line was bought and rebuilt by Pat Collins as part of his amusement park. By 1950 it was carrying up to 1,200 passengers per day. Closed and lifted in 1962, the line has since been recreated in Cleethorpes.

SUTTON MINIATURE RAILWAY, PAT COLLINS AMUSEMENT PARK, CRYSTAL PALACE, SUTTON COLDFIELD

△ CW Bartholomew's private 15in gauge line, built in 1903 for his estate at Blakesley Hall, in Northamptonshire, carried supplies, and sometimes passengers – as this Edwardian card indicates. The line closed in the late 1930s.

◁ Lord Gretton, a miniature railway enthusiast, built a long line around his estate at Stapleford Hall, near Melton Mowbray, in 1958. This card, sent in 1963, shows him at the controls of 'John of Gaunt' at the Lakeside terminus.

◁ This Edwardian card shows the Bricket Wood railway built by GE Flooks in about 1903, near St Alban's. Bricket Wood became famous for its funfairs in the late Victorian era.

Geo. E. Flooks' Miniature Railway, "Woodside," Bricket Wood, near St. Alban's.

▷ The Duke of Westminster built an estate railway to serve Eaton Hall, in Cheshire, in 1896. Primarily for supplies, it also carried passengers to and from the local mainline station.

Miniature Railway, Eaton, Chester

151

ENGINEERING MODELS

ENGINEERS HAVE MADE SCALE MODELS of railway locomotives at least since the 1840s, usually highly detailed, working replicas of contemporary engines. This custom grew steadily over the late Victorian period, thanks in part to the growth in railway enthusiasm. Amateur engineering was encouraged by clubs and societies, along with the increasing availability of handbooks, published plans and components made by professional suppliers.

In the 20th century, railway modelling became ever more popular, with modellers often making replicas of historic, as well as contemporary, locomotives, in scales from 0 gauge to 10in and above.

◀ Many specialist engineering companies published locomotive plans and blueprints for modellers. This plan, for an LB&SC tank locomotive, is in a 1938 catalogue from G Kennion & Co of London.

▼ In a rare conjunction, the model meets the real thing. The famous LMS Pacific 'Princess Elizabeth' dwarfs a fine scale model, posed rather precariously on a ganger's trolley.

▲ Magazines aimed at the model engineer included *The Model Railway Constructor*. This is the May 1935 issue.

▼ Bond's of Euston Road, London, was a famous name in model engineering. Their range included finished models, kits and components for rail and maritime modellers. This is their 1938 catalogue.

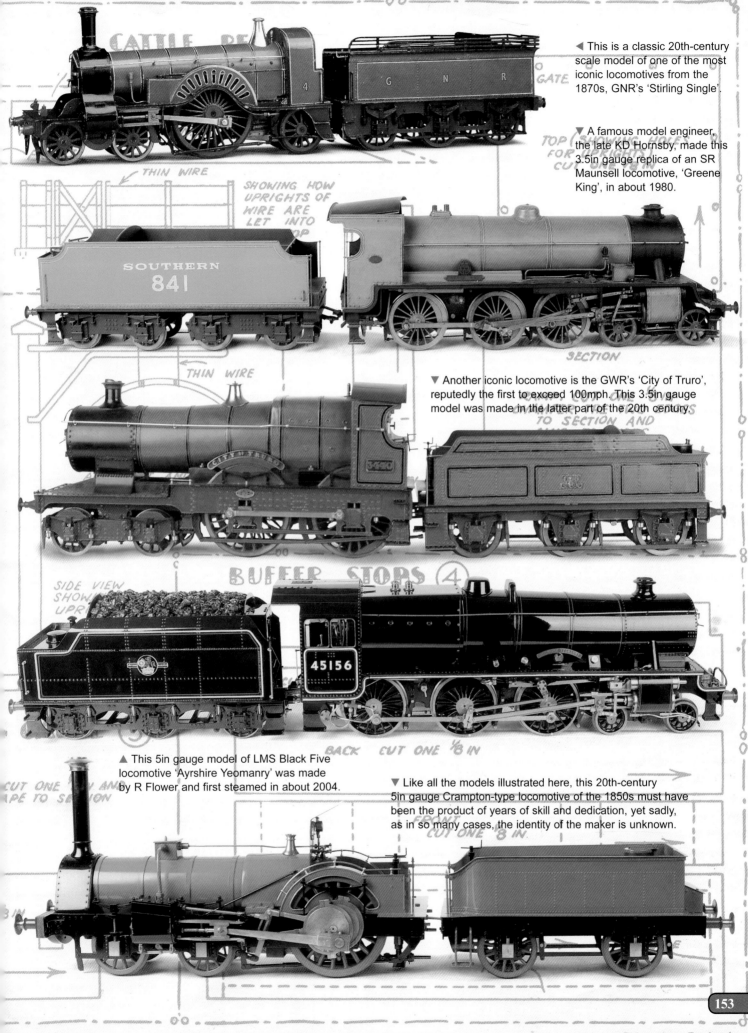

◄ This is a classic 20th-century scale model of one of the most iconic locomotives from the 1870s, GNR's 'Stirling Single'.

▼ A famous model engineer, the late KD Hornsby, made this 3.5in gauge replica of an SR Maunsell locomotive, 'Greene King', in about 1980.

▼ Another iconic locomotive is the GWR's 'City of Truro', reputedly the first to exceed 100mph. This 3.5in gauge model was made in the latter part of the 20th century.

▲ This 5in gauge model of LMS Black Five locomotive 'Ayrshire Yeomanry' was made by R Flower and first steamed in about 2004.

▼ Like all the models illustrated here, this 20th-century 5in gauge Crampton-type locomotive of the 1850s must have been the product of years of skill and dedication, yet sadly, as in so many cases, the identity of the maker is unknown.

Printed in England

EAST ANGLIA

THE SHERINGHAM BRANCH

U NTIL THE 1960s Norfolk had a remarkably comprehensive railway network, despite the rural nature of the county. Its creation, during the latter part of the 19th century, involved a surprising number of small, independent companies. The first line to Cromer was opened by the East Norfolk Railway in 1877. Ten years later another line, built by the Eastern & Midlands Railway, reached the town via Sheringham, helping to put Cromer and the north Norfolk coast on the tourist map. In 1883 this and several other companies were merged into the Midland & Great Northern Joint Railway, a famously idiosyncratic company with smart brown locomotives and a network of 183 miles, much of it single track. In 1923 the M&GNR became part of the LNER, and carried on until most of it was obliterated in 1959. All that survived of north Norfolk's network was the line from Norwich to Sheringham via Cromer.

◁ One of the many pleasures of the modern journey from Norwich to Sheringham is Worstead station, a delightful survivor from the days of the East Norfolk Railway and the GER, which took it over in 1881. It is a classic rural station, with delicate ironwork and a retired signal box.

▽ In 1997 the line became a Community Partnership railway, renamed the Bittern Line. This leaflet was published to launch the Bittern Line Partnership. Previously, British Rail had promoted the route as part of Britain's Scenic Railway.

▷ In the Edwardian era the stations were smart and substantial, catering for both freight and increasing passenger traffic. Yet, on this sunny day at Salhouse, there was plenty of time for the staff to pose and for the photographer to stand on the tracks to take his picture.

◁ In 1968, but in a setting with echoes, and structures, of an earlier era in railway history, a DMU from Norwich approaches Cromer.

▽ In the summer of 1979 a Norwich-bound DMU waits to depart from Cromer. This was where the M&GNJR and the GER met, and today, with Cromer's other station closed and with no through route, it is a terminus, compelling trains to reverse out.

S. 12759. West Runton Hotel and Station

(16)
MIDLAND & GREAT NORTHERN RAILWAYS
JOINT COMMITTEE.

TO

West Runton

◁ When this card was printed early in the 20th century, West Runton was becoming a smart little resort village on the north Norfolk coast. Unlike many similar little stations that were scattered all over Norfolk, this one still has a train service.

◁ Today, Sheringham's mainline station is beyond the crossing gates, which were removed when the line west of here was closed in the 1960s. The original Sheringham station, behind the camera, was cut off and abandoned until brought back to life by the preserved North Norfolk Railway. At some point the crossing is to be reinstated, allowing occasional trains to run through from Norwich to Holt.

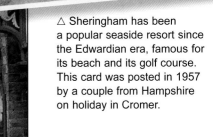

(18—V19)

MIDLAND & GREAT NORTHERN RAILWAYS JOINT COMMITTEE.

TO

Sheringham

◁ Today, the end of the line from Norwich is a minimal station, but the Community Rail Partnership makes the most of it. More importantly, the line is well used, as this photograph shows, with plenty of people awaiting a weekday mid-morning service, operated by a modern Class 156 two-carriage DMU set.

WEST PROMENADE AND BEACH, SHERINGHAM.

K.5913

△ Sheringham has been a popular seaside resort since the Edwardian era, famous for its beach and its golf course. This card was posted in 1957 by a couple from Hampshire on holiday in Cromer.

◁ The North Norfolk Railway, or the Poppy Line, operates steam trains between Sheringham and Holt. In so doing it keeps alive a small part of the old M&GNJR network – and the traditions of that company and its successors, the LNER and British Railways. Here, in the summer of 2008, a promotional film is being made on the platform at Sheringham's old and richly decorated station.

THE STOKE FERRY BRANCH

IN 1882 THE DOWNHAM & STOKE FERRY Railway was opened. Independently built but operated by the Great Eastern, this 7-mile line branched off the King's Lynn main line at Denver, 1.5 miles south of Downham Market. Serving a remote agricultural region, passenger services were always limited, and the branch was one of the first to employ conductor guards who, from 1895, issued tickets on the trains. In the 1923 Grouping, the line became part of the LNER, which gave up passenger carrying on the branch in 1930. However, freight traffic had always been more substantial, particularly after 1905, when the Wissington Light Railway, branching away to the south near Abbey, opened its extensive agricultural network. This, over 18 miles at its peak, kept part of the line open until 1982 for the carriage of sugar beet to the Wissington sugar factory, opened in 1924. Other freight traffic had been abandoned by British Railways in 1965.

▷ There were two intermediate stations, at Ryston and Abbey. This is Ryston, on a typically quiet day. The station house survives today, with the platform and parts of the level crossing. All the railway's buildings were in a distinctive architectural style, the cream brickwork relieved with bands of red.

△ In this Edwardian card a train draws into Stoke Ferry station at the end of the line, with passengers waiting for the return service to Denver, on the main King's Lynn line.

▷ Ryston station today reveals much of its railway past. The crossing gates survive, one completely subsumed into a hedge, and the station house, now private, remains along with the platform. There was a big station yard, busy with animal and other agricultural traffic.

▽ In the 1950s two men pass the time of day on the platform at Abbey station, a few miles south of the village it served, West Dereham. They cannot be waiting for a train as passenger services had ceased in 1930, so they are probably railway enthusiasts. Today, the station house survives, but there is no sign of any track.

G. E. R.

From _____

TO

STOKE FERRY

◁ A charming Edwardian postcard, complete with carefully posed child, shows the substantial nature of Stoke Ferry station. Sadly, it never fulfilled the expectations of the line's local promoters.

▷ ▽ Today, Stoke Ferry station still stands, along with its platform, goods shed and other buildings, but its future is uncertain as the entire site is likely to be developed. Behind the station building (right) is the station master's house, visible to the right on the postcard above. The goods shed (below) is on the left of the card. The buildings are a good example of the particular brickwork style used by the Downham & Stoke Ferry Railway, the independent builders of the branch.

◁ There are many traceable remains of the Wissington Light Railway and the sugar beet trade. One example is this concrete bridge over the river Denver, a modern structure that indicates the continuing importance of the line to the sugar industry into the early 1980s.

▽ Remote branches and little-used lines threatened with closure were frequently included on the routes of enthusiasts' railtours during the 1950s and 1960s. These often resulted in the use of the largest trains the lines had ever seen. Typical is this view of the Eastern Counties special, which had arrived at Stoke Ferry in 1959 with a train far longer than the platform.

163

THE UPWELL TRAMWAY

When it opened in 1884 the Wisbech & Upwell Railway was a rare British example of a roadside tramway, a type of low-cost railway much more common in Europe. Built and operated by the Great Eastern, the 6-mile line enjoyed a long and profitable life, especially for freight, becoming part of the LNER empire and then British Railways. The LNER gave up passenger services in January 1928, but freight lived on until May 1966. Being classed as a roadside tramway, the line was known for its unusual locomotives and passenger vehicles, one of which survives. Between 1883 and 1921 the GER built a series of distinctive tram engines for the line and, in 1930, a couple of special Sentinels. Even British Railways responded to the railway's unusual nature with a pair of special Drewry diesels in 1952. Very little remains to be seen today.

◁ A freight and a passenger train pass at Boyce's Bridge, one of four stops between Wisbech and Upwell, on a snowy day in the 1920s.

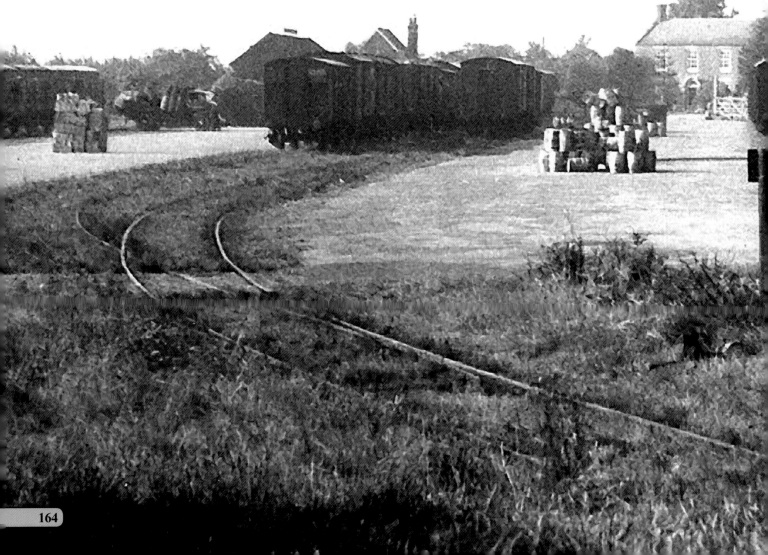

Steam Tram, Wisbech

◁ This old postcard shows the roadside nature of the tramway and illustrates one of the specially built tram locomotives with enclosed wheels for safety. The rather random nature of the carriages is also apparent. Some went on to other lives elsewhere after the end of passenger services in 1928.

P 0389
G.E.R.
WISBECH & OUTWELL TRAMWAY
1ᴰ Third Class 1

K 0295
G.E.R.
WISBECH & OUTWELL TRAMWAY
2ᴰ Third Class 2

Z 9813
G.E.R.
WISBECH & OUTWELL TRAMWAY
3ᴰ Third Class 3
WISBECH to UPWELL

K 9560
G.E.R.
WISBECH & OUTWELL TRAMWAY
4ᴰ First Class 4
UPWELL to WISBECH

▽ The steam tram stands ready to depart from a bay platform at Wisbech station, but there is still time for everyone to pose for the photographer, who – as so often used to be the case – is standing on the track.

S 6546   STEAM TRAM IN WISBECH STATION.

◁ The end of the line, Upwell, probably in the 1930s: the tracks are almost hidden in the grass and the facilities are minimal, but there is plenty of assorted freight traffic to keep the line busy.

△ After closure in 1966 the Wisbech & Upwell Tramway quickly disappeared as its roadside route became buried beneath road widening and other local changes. It can be explored by car or on foot, and occasionally the trackbed can be identified, but overall it really is a lost railway. This garden centre sits squarely on the route of the trackbed, but at least its name commemorates the railway.

▷ It is the mid-1960s and the line is soon to close, but the trains are still running, just. One of the special Drewry diesels takes a minimal freight train – one open wagon and the guard's van – across Elm Road, on a typically ungated crossing.

◁ This is the remains of Elm Bridge station in the 1960s. Even in the days of regular passenger services the facilities were fairly basic. Carriages had steps and balconies at the ends, to help access.

▷ Freight was the key to the railway's success over a long period. Here, in the 1920s, one of the railway's Edwardian tram locomotives brings a long line of box wagons alongside a residential road on the outskirts of Wisbech.

THE THAXTED BRANCH

A TYPICAL PRODUCT of the Light Railways Act of 1896, the Elsenham & Thaxted Light Railway was a wholly local venture, although the Great Eastern had an interest and ran the line. Always under-financed, the railway, authorized in 1906, was not completed until April 1913. At just over 5 miles long, and with no engineering features of significance, it was simply built and operated. There was a speed limit of 25mph, and the line ended well short of Thaxted. Not surprisingly, it had a quiet life, and in 1949 there were six trains each way on weekdays only. In September 1952 passenger services ceased, and the branch was closed completely the following June, having survived for just over 40 years. Today, there is little to be seen in the undulating Essex countryside.

▽ The most visible survivor of the Elsenham & Thaxted Light Railway is a length of low embankment near the site of Sibley's station (or, to give it its full name, Sibley's for Chickney and Broxted). Though overgrown and rather inaccessible, part of this is a footpath.

△ The branch ended about a mile short of Thaxted village, virtually in the middle of nowhere, and the terminus station was a plain timber structure. The engine shed, seen here in 1952, was more substantial.

L N E R
B 877
LUGGAGE
From LIVERPOOL STREET
To THAXTED

▽ The branch left the main Liverpool Street-to-Cambridge line at Elsenham, a quiet country station seen here in the 1920s. Thaxted trains left from a bay platform, to the right of the station building.

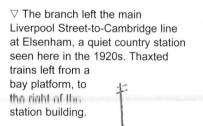

◁ There were four intermediate stations on the line, and the journey took about 20 minutes. The stations were all extremely rudimentary, and two, Culter's Green Halt and Henham Halt (shown here) were formed from old carriage bodies.

BRITISH RAILWAYS

ELSENHAM AND THAXTED BRANCH LINE
WITHDRAWAL OF PASSENGER TRAIN SERVICE

The Railway Executive hereby give notice that on and from 15th September 1952 the passenger train service will be withdrawn from the undermentioned stations and halts on the Elsenham-Thaxted Branch:

MILL ROAD HALT   CUTLER'S GREEN HALT
HENHAM HALT   THAXTED
SIBLEY'S

An omnibus service will be provided by the Eastern National Omnibus Company between Bishop's Stortford Elsenham and Thaxted

Facilities for the handling of coal merchandise and parcels traffic will continue to be available at Elsenham Sibley's and Thaxted stations until further notice

△ Thaxted is a famously attractive village, with the grand medieval guildhall and the church with its tall spire at its centre. In this 1920s postcard, the streets are more or less deserted. It is a pity the railway never actually reached the town.

▽ This shows the stretch of low embankment near Sibley's, rising above a field of broad beans. The large pillbox is an imposing reminder of one of the many lines of defence drawn across the English landscape in 1940.

SCRAPBOOK : EAST ANGLIA

DESPITE THE RELATIVELY SMALL population and the lack of heavy industry, East Anglia was being criss-crossed by railways from the 1840s. Most were built by small companies with local concerns, but the main trunk routes and connections to London, the Midlands and the North were soon in place. In 1862 many of the small companies were formed into the Great Eastern Railway, and this dominated the region until the Grouping of 1923 created the LNER. The East Anglian railways were characterized by branch lines and rural routes, some of which came together as the Midland & Great Northern Junction, whose network ranged from Lincolnshire across north Norfolk. Inevitably, much of the region's network was closed from the 1950s.

▷ In the 1960s railways often worked closely with airlines to promote excursions. This 1962 British Railways handbill advertises pre-Stansted, no-passport day trips to the Continent. A day trip to Calais cost £4.7s (£4.35).

BRITISH RAILWAYS

DAY ON THE CONTINENT
WITH AND WITHOUT PASSPORTS

BY RAIL AND AIR

from LONDON (Liverpool Street)
CAMBRIDGE
BISHOP'S STORTFORD
HARLOW
STRATFORD
ILFORD
ROMFORD
SHENFIELD
IPSWICH
COLCHESTER
CHELMSFORD
via ROCHFORD and SOUTHEND AIRPORT

SPEND A WHOLE DAY IN CALAIS or OSTEND

DAILY from 1st JULY 1962
until further notice

▽ This publicity photograph shows the final preparations and last-minute polishing for a railway exhibition organized by the LNER at Southend station in May 1933. The display ranged from industrial locomotives to giants such as the 'Flying Scotsman' and Class W1, No. 10000, Gresley's famous experimental locomotive and the first on the LNER to be streamlined.

◁ Station gardens were always popular, and the LNER took the annual competitions very seriously. This is Haverhill, on the Cambridge-to-Marks Tey line, probably in the 1950s, with a fine example of a station name in white-painted stones.

▷ A rare survivor is the branch line to Southminster in Essex. Today, this is a busy commuter route, but in the 1950s Althorne, near Burnham-on-Crouch, was a sleepy rural station, and there was always time for children to watch the trains.

△ The Southminster route is today fully electrified and has lost some of the branchline quality that can be seen in this 1964 photograph, even though the line was then operated by modern three-car DMU units. On this autumn day Southminster was very quiet, with no passengers waiting and just one or two cars in the parking area.

A LONG DAY
on the
NORFOLK COAST

WEDNESDAYS,
13th, 20th, 27th JULY 3rd,
10th, 17th, 24th & 31st AUGUST.

SATURDAYS,
16th and 23rd JULY, 1927.

CHEAP TRIPS
to
WELLS-ON-SEA

SPECIAL LATE TRAIN
On the above dates a SPECIAL LATE TRAIN
will leave WELLS-ON-SEA at 8.30 p.m. for
DEREHAM, calling at intermediate stations.
TAKE YOUR TICKETS IN ADVANCE.

LNER

◁ The LNER was an efficient excursion operator, with its eye on promoting such lesser-used lines as the former GER route from Dereham to Wells. This handbill dates from 1927.

▷ In 1956 the driver brings his push-pull train into the deserted platform at Paston & Knapton station on the North Walsham-to-Mundesley line, a surviving fragment of the coastal route to Cromer, which closed in 1953.

Parham Station.

MIDLAND & GREAT NORTHERN JOINT
RAILWAY PRESERVATION SOCIETY

East Anglia needs:—

RAILWAYS
NOT ROADS

This Society has been formed to PRESERVE YOUR RAILWAY. The first sections to be attempted will be:—

1 Melton Constable to Norwich City.
2 Aylsham North to North Walsham Town.
3 North Walsham to Yarmouth Beach.

Although it is planned to use parts of the latter section as a road it is still possible to open it as a railway. It is also intended to re-open, at a later date, the sections Peterborough to Sutton Bridge, and Bourne to Sutton Bridge.

To achieve this we must have YOUR SUPPORT NOW.

Full details may be had from, Mr. R. P. Thomas, 7 Sunny Hill, NORWICH, Norfolk, NOR. 69C.

If possible please enclose a 3d. stamp when writing.

Remember, East Anglia needs RAILWAYS NOT ROADS.

DONT DELAY, JOIN TO-DAY

△ Most of the former M&GN lines in Norfolk were closed in 1959, but not without protests – as this leaflet indicates. At that time, the 'Railways Not Roads' slogan was doomed to failure; today, it would be a different story.

△ ▷ The East Suffolk Railway, an 1850s amalgam of various local lines, was also a busy branchline builder. Typical was the line to Framlingham from Wickham Market, opened in 1859, just as this network was absorbed into the Eastern Counties Railway. Later, it all became part of the GER, and then the LNER. The Framlingham branch, an essentially local affair, was an early closure, with passenger services ending in November 1952. There were three intermediate stations, one of which was Parham, seen above in some idyllic 1920s summer, with children playing around the river. For a minor line, the station was quite grand. The photograph to the right shows the terminus at Framlingham, not long before the line closed.

◁ In December 1960 the Ipswich-bound, two-car DMU accelerates away from Darsham, on the East Suffolk line, into the winter afternoon. A single passenger crosses the railway tracks, bringing home, as the caption puts it, 'the Christmas cheer'.

▽ It is the 1960s and the East Anglian railway network is being decimated by closures. Maybe this Vauxhall was part of an experiment aimed at putting cars on the tracks after the trains had gone – giving a new meaning to the word 'railcar'. Whatever is happening, there is much discussion, while the DMU driver bides his time.

▷ The first station at Ipswich was a temporary terminus opened in 1847. The through station was built in 1860 for the Eastern Counties Railway, later absorbed into the Great Eastern. The island platform, with its decorative awning, was added in 1883. This view dates from Great Eastern days, but the station today is still much the same.

◁ Cheap tickets for use on market days used to be issued in many parts of Britain. This 1949 British Railways handbill lists Market Tickets for a number of East Anglian stations.

▷ Traffic on the Suffolk Coast line, a rural route from Ipswich to Lowestoft, was often encouraged by excursions, tours and other promotional offers. These BR leaflets are from 1963 and 1972.

△ This Edwardian card shows the Suffolk station of Beccles in its heyday, when the main line from Ipswich to Great Yarmouth had connections to Norwich and Lowestoft.

▷ It was the Norfolk Railway that turned Lowestoft from a remote fishing town into a major resort, and the Central station, built from 1847, was a suitably substantial structure. This 1960s view gives an idea of the scale of the station, much of which was demolished in 1992.

▽ Worstead, near North Walsham, is still a station on the line from Norwich to Sheringham, but it was looking rather more important when this photograph was taken in about 1910 than it does today.

△ The railway reached Cromer in 1877, at a station away from the town centre. More central was Cromer Beach, opened in 1887. However, Cromer High, seen here, remained in use as a terminus and for freight. On this day in the 1950s the only activity is a porter transferring parcels from a box van onto a flatbed Bedford lorry.

MILITARY RAILWAYS

Britain's network of military railways was started by the Victorians, but the major development occurred during the two world wars, with many camps, dockyards, airfields and depots being rail-connected. At its peak, the network covered hundreds of miles of lines and sidings across Britain, served by numbers of stations, most not accessible to the public. The primary traffic for military railways was stores and equipment. The movement of troops and service personnel was also important, though many travelled on scheduled services with special tickets and warrants.

▲ This typical travel warrant, issued by the Great Northern Railway of Ireland, was for a soldier travelling from Belfast to Banbury in 1944, perhaps for the D-Day preparations.

◀ Large numbers of American locomotives came to Britain in 1944 for use by the US Army Transportation Corps. This example was working at Southampton docks. Some subsequently served with British Railways.

◀ A military line from Brookwood served several camps – Bisley, Pirbright, Deepcut and Blackdown. After World War II much of the line was closed, and Bisley became the terminus. This shows the 'Bisley Bullet', the popular name for the British Railways train that served the route, in July 1952, a few days before closure. The pavilion-like station building survives.

▼ A branch from Ludgershall, on the old Midland & South Western Junction line, served Tidworth and, later, Tidworth Camp. This shows the once-busy station in virtual disuse, shortly before closure in 1963.

4237 G.W.R.
TO
Ludgershall

▼ This early 20th-century view of Tidworth shows the station, and in the background the sprawl of the military camp and the open landscape so loved by the military.

0675
SOUTHERN RAILWAY.
Issued subject to the Bye-laws,
Regulations & Conditions in the
Company's Bills and Notices.
OFFICER ON LEAVE
to NEW CROSS
Via
First Class L
NOT TRANSFERABLE.
SOUTHERN RAILWAY.
OFFICER ON LEAVE
New Cross to
Via
First Class
0675

▼ Lydd Camp was on a military branch from Lydd Town, on the Appledore-to-Dungeness branch in Kent. The ordnance and the uniforms suggest this is an Edwardian view.

M&SW JT STATION TIDWORTH 1872

◀ A group of soldiers cluster on the platform of a station somewhere in Southwest England, ready to entrain, perhaps en route to service during World War I. Friends and family have come to say their farewells.

The Camp, Lydd.

R.F.A. at Trawsfynydd Station

◀ This colourful Edwardian card shows the Royal Field Artillery at Trawsfynydd station, on the Bala-to-Blaenau Ffestiniog line, in central Wales, a popular area for military exercises at the time. This was a public station, and locals, clustered round the locomotives, have obviously turned out in force to watch.

◀ The Longmoor Military Railway, which ran from Bordon to Liss, in Hampshire, was used primarily for training purposes. Generations of army engineers gained experience on operations here. It was famous for its annual open days, which attracted enthusiasts in large numbers.

▶ Longmoor's star was the WD 2-10-0 locomotive 'Gordon', seen here in action in the 1960s, and since preserved. The railway closed in 1969.

The transport of military equipment was a major railway activity. This shows Woodburn station, Northumberland, on the line from Morpeth to Reedsmouth, in the mid-1960s. This was not a military station, but it handled a lot of military traffic as it was the railhead for the nearby Otterburn ranges, the destination for this cargo of guns and lorries.

Tin Town Mail.

▲ The military association with Tidworth started in 1897, but before there was much military development an isolation hospital was built at Brimstone Bottom. This, known as 'Tin Town', from the huts built for the hospital and its workforce, was served by trains on the Tidworth branch from 1901.

◄ One of Britain's more obscure military railways ran from Kilnsea Fort to Spurn Point, on the Humber estuary. Opened in 1915, it was used by naval personnel and the local lighthouse crew, and survived until 1951. It was famous for the diversity of its motive power, including various steam engines and petrol-powered vehicles, notably an old Itala racing car adapted to run on rails and a sail-powered trolley. This shows the Kilnsea terminus in 1950.

FARMING, FISHING & FERRIES

EAST ANGLIA'S MAIN INDUSTRY has always been agriculture, so the building of the region's railway network reflected that. Such heavy industry as there was often related to agriculture too. The railways also served the major fishing ports, notably Lowestoft and Great Yarmouth. Indeed, it was the early development of dedicated fish traffic to London from East Anglia that modernized the marketing of fish. The ports too were important. Some, such as Ipswich, Harwich, Wisbech and King's Lynn, expanded greatly with the coming of the railway; others, for example Tilbury and Felixstowe, were created by the railway. Also railway-linked was a series of small coastal and river ports and harbours.

◁ Encroaching vegetation on the March-to-Wisbech line suggests it was closed years ago, but the sign and crossing gates indicate otherwise.

▽ Old British Rail wagon labels reflect the range of freight and dock traffic that used to be a part of the East Anglian railway scene.

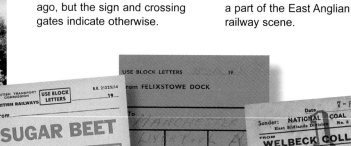

▽ Although it closed to passengers in 1968, the March-to-Wisbech line remained open for goods traffic until 2001. It served Wisbech docks, local agriculture and various industries, including a pet-food factory. Track and infrastructure remain in place, as this modern photograph of the river crossing at Chainbridge shows, and there are plans to reopen the line to passengers.

△ There were several rail-operated industrial sites in East Anglia. This 0-4-0 locomotive was working at the Manganese Bronze & Brass Company's sidings at Ipswich in the 1930s.

△ Posted in 1908, this card gives an idea of the scale and diversity of activity in the docks at King's Lynn. These remained in railway operation until relatively recently.

◁ Dock networks were often connected to the main line by street railways, giving rise to scenes like this. Here, an LNER tram engine shunts wagons in Ipswich docks, probably in the late 1930s or 1940s.

◁ The mainstay of international freight traffic was the train ferry, and scheduled services to the Continent operated from a number of British ports. One of the largest, and one of the last to remain in operation, was Harwich. The port is still used for passenger traffic.

▽ Little ports all around the coast of Britain found a new lease of life with the coming of the railways, and quayside lines such as this, at Wells-next-the-Sea in the 1920s, were a common sight.

THE POPULARITY of east coast resorts grew rapidly at the start of the 20th century. This inspired the building of a number of miniature railways, and some important lines opened in the 1920s and 1930s. Much more unusual in eastern England were narrow gauge railways. Apart from quarry and mineral lines, the only significant narrow gauge line to carry passengers was the famous Southwold Railway.

YARMOUTH MINIATURE RAILWAY
YARMOUTH BELLE ARRIVING AT 8TH. DENES JUNCTN.
PHOTO HOBBS
GT. YARMOUTH

MINIATURE RAILWAY, HUNSTANTON

◁ A miniature railway was laid along the pier at Hunstanton, Norfolk, in the 1930s and survived in various forms until the 1960s. This card shows the line, and an empty pier, in the 1950s. The locomotive may be a Bassett-Lowke of about 1928. Storms destroyed the pier in 1978, along with any traces of the railway.

△ Great Yarmouth had a very grand miniature railway between 1929 and 1937. It had enclosed coaches, a station with an island platform and overbridge, and a named train, 'The Yarmouth Belle'. There was even a 'dining car', serving drinks and biscuits. This 1930 card shows the main station, South Denes. Note the maintenance train on the left.

▽ A happy young passenger poses in front of the miniature Stirling Single locomotive that was one of the features of the 18in gauge Jaywick Sands Railway, near Clacton-on-Sea, Essex. Smart coaches with electric light and a tunnel on the route were other hallmarks of this short-lived line, in operation from 1936 until the outbreak of World War II.

◁ This 1930s card shows the miniature railway at Jaywick Sands, Essex, in its heyday. Its three bogie coaches and the Stirling-style locomotive wait at Crossways station in the Tudor village. The number of parked cars suggests there was no shortage of passengers.

△ Pressure from local residents brought the Southwold Railway into existence. From 1879 to 1929 it was this smart little Suffolk resort's main link to the outside world. The 3ft gauge line followed an attractive route along the river Blyth, and the intermediate stations included Walberswick, seen here in 1910.

▽ Following some years of financial decline, the last train left Southwold on the evening of 11 April 1929. Track, infrastructure and rolling stock was simply abandoned and lay derelict while nature encroached, as this 1930s photograph indicates. Nothing happened until 1941, when everything was cut up as scrap for the war effort.

△ The Southwold Railway was distinctive in every way, from its Sharp Stewart locomotives to its generous six-wheeled carriages, seen here at the Southwold terminus. The railway met the GER's main line at Halesworth.

MODELS & MODELMAKERS

FINELY DETAILED SCALE MODELS of railway locomotives have been made since the 1840s, usually hand-built to a remarkable standard by both amateur and professional engineers. All over the country there are clubs with demonstration tracks in various gauges, most commonly from 0 to 7.5in, on which the models – normally live steam – can be put through their paces. In many instances, raised tracks enable drivers to ride on their locomotives and haul passenger carriers. The close relationship between man and machine is apparent.

◄ 'Lady Margaret', a 7.25in gauge model of an industrial locomotive built in 1986 by D Munday, a Yorkshire model engineer, simmers quietly on the turntable at the Myddle Wood Railway.

▼ The boundaries between clubs and permanent miniature railways are ill-defined. This smoky scene shows a locomotive called 'Trojan' making the most of the 10in gauge track at the Saltwood Railway in 1960.

▶ Cigarette-smoking and overalled, this archetypal 1950s model-railway engineer tries out his GWR County Class locomotive No. 1023, 'County of Oxford'.

◄ With smoke and steam concealing both locomotive and driver, a model forces its way along the snow-covered track at a club somewhere in Britain in the 1970s.

▲ The driver's excitement and the slightly more measured enjoyment of his young passengers are apparent as this large-scale model of Southern Railway locomotive No. 787 is put through its paces.

▲ At this level, railway modelling seems to require total dedication. These two men, one wearing his BR driver's cap, are absorbed in the preparation of an LMS Royal Scot, while a passing enthusiast takes time to enjoy the scene – and his ice cream.

◄ Railway modelling would seem to be a male-dominated activity, yet this young girl in her 1970s clothes seems quite at home driving this fine model of a 5800 Class GWR tank locomotive.

NORTHERN ENGLAND

BISHOP AUCKLAND & THE WEARDALE RAILWAY

TRAINS STILL RUN from Darlington to Bishop Auckland, along one of the national network's oldest and more obscure branches. The history is complicated, with the first part of the line opened to Crook by the Stockton & Darlington Railway in 1843. Two years later the Weardale Extension Railway took the line on to Bishop Auckland, mainly for the mineral traffic. Next came the Wear Valley Railway, which extended it to Frosterley in 1847. The Frosterley & Stanhope Railway completed the next section in 1862. The final section to

Wearhead had to wait until 1895, by which time the whole line was under the control of the NER. Passenger traffic north of Bishop Auckland had gone by 1965, but the section to Eastgate remained open for cement and stone traffic until 1993. Now, the preserved Weardale Railway runs trains from Wolsingham to Stanhope.

▽ Today, the branch ends at a small modern building lost in a car park, with no hint of the grand, complicated station that once served Bishop Auckland. To add insult to injury, part of it is a driving school. On the left is the overgrown freight line that served the cement works.

◁ For a brief period from the 1980s British Rail ran scheduled summer excursions on the line from Darlington to Eastgate, including the 19-mile freight-only section northwest from Bishop Auckland.

◁ On a misty summer evening, the two-coach DMU from Darlington nears the end of the line at Bishop Auckland. In the foreground, the former mineral line to Eastgate, now isolated, branches off to the right of the photograph.

⊲ In the 1960s Bishop Auckland was the meeting point for five lines, and the station, unusual in its triangular layout, was substantial. Now, all that remains is a minimal terminus.

NORTH EASTERN RAILWAY.
Bishop Auckland.

▽ In 1967 steam was still to be seen on the Bishop Auckland line. Here, in the summer of that year, 62005 heads a train along the branch.

BRITISH RAILWAYS (Amended Issue from 13th September)

MID-WEEK OVERNIGHT TICKETS
available for return up to 17 days
AT SPECIALLY REDUCED FARES

DARLINGTON
BISHOP AUCKLAND
STOCKTON   49/-
MIDDLESBROUGH
WEST HARTLEPOOL

SUNDERLAND
SOUTH SHIELDS   52/6
DURHAM
NEWCASTLE

every TUESDAY WEDNESDAY and THURSDAY
until further notice

from KING'S CROSS dep. 11.55 p.m.

Tuesdays and Wednesdays until 16th December and from 25th December (Sleeping berths only) by advanced booking   1.0 a.m.

available for return by trains shown overleaf on or before the 17th day but only on Tuesdays, Wednesdays and Thursdays

SPECIAL BOOKING ARRANGEMENTS
22nd December to 31st December
Bookings for journeys during the period 22nd to 31st December inclusive must be made not less than 36 hours in advance, i.e. 11.0 a.m. on the day prior to travel, at :
KING'S CROSS Main Line Booking Office
LIVERPOOL STREET Main Line Booking Office
BRITISH RAILWAYS OFFICE, 110 Victoria Street, S.W.1 and
BRITISH RAILWAYS TRAVEL CENTRE, Lower Regent Street, S.W.1 or at other Eastern Region stations and ticket agencies in the London area
The dates of both outward and return journeys must be specified at the time of booking and tickets will be valid for use only on those days

The service on 24th December is subject to alteration and intending passengers should enquire as to the service available on this date

△ This 1959 handbill shows that Bishop Auckland was then an important destination for passengers from London.

△ Witton Park viaduct over the Wear was built in 1853 to replace an earlier timber bridge. Now quiet and extensively wooded, this was a busy ironworks area. The bridge abutting the viaduct carries the road.

Bishop Auckland
Bishop of Durham's Palace   Deer House in Bishop's Park

△ This card, posted in 1904, shows two of Bishop Auckland's famous features. The writer, sending the card to a friend in Middleton-in-Teesdale, says he is leaving Auckland on the 12.35.

N. E. R.

FROM DARLINGTON N.R.

FROSTERLEY

Stop
Look
Listen
Beware
of trains

△ Anyone using this footpath across the track today would be waiting for a train for ever. Most walkers just stroll along the track.

△ The mineral line from Bishop Auckland to Eastgate closed in 1993, but everything remains in place – track, signals and notices, giving it the feeling of a time warp. This is near Witton-le-Wear.

▷ At Witton-le-Wear the station has now gone, but the crossing-keeper's cottage and the crossing gates remain. Also to be seen is the ground frame, complete with its brass lever-identification plaques.

▷ The Weardale Railway reopened the section from Wolsingham to Stanhope in 2004 as a preserved line, and there are plans to extend this to Eastgate, the terminus of the former freight line. Seen here is Eastgate station, which is now a private house. The track continues westwards from here for half a mile to the former cement works that kept the line busy from 1964 to 1993.

▽ West of Eastgate the line quickly vanishes, but its route alongside the river Wear is easily traced in the landscape, though much is on private land. Near Ludwell the railway line can be seen, and explored, as a low embankment running across the fields.

△ Near Westgate the line of the railway can be seen from the road bridge. Here, a tractor sits abandoned on the embankment. Westgate station survives as a private house.

▷ Sometimes old concrete crossing-gate posts, now left isolated in the landscape, conveniently mark the route of the railway. Handsome stone bridges also survive.

◁ This Edwardian photograph shows Wearhead station not long after its opening in 1895. Passenger services ceased in 1953, with freight living on for a few years. Today, the station building, seen here in the distance, survives, along with its clock and the adjacent station house. Both are private houses. At this point the Weardale Way follows the former trackbed for a while.

Wear and Station from Bridge, Wearhead

◁ The journey along the valley of the Wear must have been a scenic one, as this view of the curving trackbed near Westgate indicates.

△ This Edwardian card shows Wearhead station from the other direction, seen from the Wear road bridge in the town. Today, the setting is completely overshadowed by trees, but the river is often just as fast-flowing.

193

THE MIDDLETON-IN-TEESDALE BRANCH

Stone and lead quarries near Middleton-in-Teesdale were the inspiration for the Tees Valley Railway. It was built from 1865 by an independent company, though with close connections to the North Eastern Railway, which operated it from the start and took it over in 1882. The route, winding for nearly 9 miles from Barnard Castle along the valley of the Tees to Middleton-in-Teesdale, was dramatic. As the mineral traffic diminished, tourism became more important, helping to keep the line in business until it was closed to passengers in November 1964. Freight lingered on for a few months. Most of the route is now the Tees Valley Railway Path.

△ From Middleton to near Cotherstone, apart from a short interruption around Romaldkirk, the trackbed is now the Tees Valley Railway Path. It is a pleasant walk, with fine views and a number of surviving bridges handsomely built from the local grey limestone.

△ Barnard Castle was the starting point for the journey and is seen here in the 1950s with the branchline train on the right. The branch followed the main line towards Stainmore for a while. Now, the site of the junction where the Middleton branch dropped down from the main line's curving embankment is hard to see.

▽ In August 1964, a few months before closure, a train waits in vain for passengers at Romaldkirk, one of three intermediate stations. Today, the station building is a private house.

▷ In 1905, when this card was posted from Barnard Castle, the terminus at Middleton was a substantial structure near the Tees and a short walk from the town. The passenger train in the platform shows how important tourism was by that date.

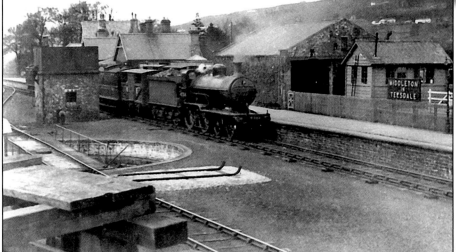

NORTH EASTERN RAILWAY.

From_____

MIDDLETON-IN-TEESDALE

◁ This later view of Middleton station includes the water tower and the turntable. Today, the station and the station house live on as part of the Daleview Caravan Park.

▽ The major engineering feature on the branch is the five-arched viaduct over the river Lune, set on a curve in a dramatic fold of hills southeast of Middleton. Built in grey limestone, with white brick lining for the arches, it is now part of the Tees Valley Railway Path.

THE CONISTON BRANCH

THE LAKE DISTRICT was famously resistant to railways. Only one line ever crossed this splendid landscape, from Penrith to Cockermouth; three branches crept into the edges. The Coniston Railway, which attacked from the south, completed its line from Foxfield, near Broughton-in-Furness, to Coniston, in 1859. Though nominally independent, it was supported, and ultimately owned, by the Furness Railway, famous for its pioneering interest in tourism.

However, the Coniston line was always limited as a Lake District gateway. A branch to local copper mines helped to keep it open, but this was not enough and it was the first Lake District line to close, in 1958.

Coniston.   Brantwood House.

△ Coniston's most famous resident was the writer and critic John Ruskin, whose last years were spent in Brantwood, a fine house overlooking the lake. It is now open to the public. Did Ruskin, a fierce opponent of railways, use the branch line?

△ There were three intermediate stations, Broughton-in-Furness, Woodland and Torver – all handsome stone structures. This is an Edwardian view of Woodland, a remarkably grand station for so remote a location. It survives as a private house, with platform intact.

▷ At Broughton-in-Furness the line passed through the centre of the town. Today, the station buildings remain, but a road now runs where the tracks went. For a short stretch just to the north, the trackbed becomes a footpath.

Railway Station,
Broughton-in-Furness.

It is hard today to follow the route of the Coniston branch for, although it is still there in the landscape, it is largely hidden and inaccessible. Bridges and other structures can be seen, mostly well built from local stone. This is a typical view of the secret world of the lost Coniston railway.

57† 5,000 | 3 | 11.

TO
CONISTON
From the Furness Railway.

◁ Coniston had a magnificent station, built on a plateau carved from solid rock high above the town and the lake. Today, it is a housing and industrial estate with few clues to its previous life. From here a short branch continued into the hills to the copper mines.

▷ This Edwardian photograph gives a sense of the station's magnificent setting. However, not much is going on and the platforms are deserted. Under-use was always a problem with the Coniston branch, prompting its early closure.

▽ In the autumn of 1958 closure was imminent. The push-pull service to Foxfield and the main line is ready to depart, but there are few passengers sheltering in the decorative train shed. It is a classic branch line scene.

▷ Near Torver the railway follows the road for a while and there is suddenly much to be seen. Sometimes it is a line of trees in the valley, and sometimes a low embankment, surprisingly well manicured and accompanied by drystone walls and the occasional bridge.

▽ Tempting though it is, the Coniston line cannot be walked. Much of it is private and inaccessible, and parts are completely lost. However, the visible sections can easily be enjoyed from adjacent roads and there are a number of highlights, such as this stretch of embankment leading to a lovely stone bridge. Beyond, there is an old platelayer's hut.

SCRAPBOOK : NORTHERN ENGLAND

THE NORTH OF ENGLAND was the birthplace of the modern railway, so its railway legacy is naturally strong. It is a region famous for freight, mainline expresses, and grand stations and structures, yet it was also rich in rural routes and branch lines. Many were the result of competition in the early years, when great railway empires came and went with surprising rapidity. Initially, those empires were driven by the needs of coal and engineering, but passengers soon came into the equation, with the development of coastal and inland resorts and their links to the towns and cities. From the 1950s both freight and passenger traffic declined, and closures removed great sections of the northern network, especially the minor lines.

Convalescent Home, Withernsea.

▷ The Hull & Holderness Railway completed its line to Withernsea in 1854. This Edwardian postcard shows the terminus station at Withernsea in the North Eastern Railway era. The imposing convalescent home was part of the town's development as an east coast resort.

▽ In evening sun a DMU waits at Withernsea in the early 1960s. The station is looking tired, and closure is threatening. The end came in October 1964.

◁ This most basic of stations is the end of a branch line that linked the remote north Lincolnshire town of Fockerby to the railway network. There is simply nothing there, and even the porter is wheeling his barrow out of the picture. This little-used railway was closed to passengers in 1933 and to freight in 1965.

▽ In an evocative railway image of the early 1960s, a freight train bound for Scarborough drifts across the magnificent Larpool viaduct. Below it are the lines leading to Whitby Town and Whitby West Cliff, parts of an east coast network now greatly diminished. Today the viaduct still stands, but the Esk Valley line to Middlesbrough is the only route to survive.

▷ The branch line to Richmond, which opened in 1846, ended in a magnificent Gothic terminus designed by GT Andrews, the greatest railway architect of this region. This shows the station's grand train shed soon after the line's closure in 1969. It has now been fully restored as a leisure complex.

▽ Ulverston's grand station is a reflection of the ambitions of its builder, the Furness Railway. Here, in 1963, small boys watch while the fireman does something energetic on the tender, and the stationmaster approaches purposefully as the train for Lancaster waits to depart.

Cockermouth, Keswick and Penrith Railway. F7695

REFER BACK TO YOUR LETTER.

Reference No. G.C. 177450

MEMO. FROM THE SECRETARY AND MANAGER,

KESWICK STATION.

To Mr Allinson, Keswick.

29th Octr, 1918.

Coward Philipson & Co o/s 1/6.

But why did you enter this through to Tean seeing that you have no rates in operation with this station. You ought to have applied for a rate for the consignment.

J. Clark, per

◁ The Cockermouth, Keswick & Penrith Railway, opened in 1865, was the only line to cross the Lake District. It was primarily a tourist line, though freight was important, as this delightfully querulous memo of 1918 indicates. The last section of the line closed in 1972.

▷ In July 1956 there has been a bit of rain at Kielder Forest, in Northumberland, a rather remote spot on the Hexham-to-Riccarton Junction via Reedsmouth Borders line, but Class V1 tank locomotive No. 67639 is immaculate and gleaming. Three months later the line closed for passengers.

▽ In 1962, when most visitors to the Lake District still travelled by train, there were several routes into the region. Gone today are lines to Coniston and from Workington to Penrith.

THE
ENGLISH LAKES
FOR YOUR 1962 HOLIDAY

COMBINED RAIL ROAD AND LAKE
TOURS HOLIDAY RUNABOUT TICKETS

EVERYTHING FOR YOUR HOLIDAY

LONDON MIDLAND

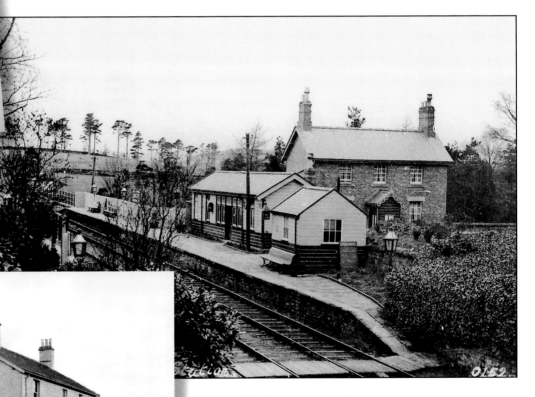

△ ◁ In 1869 the Hexham & Allendale Railway opened its line to passengers. This 12-mile branch served a remote region of Northumberland. Langley (above) was one of the three intermediate stations. Shown left is Allendale station, the end of line. It was actually nearer Catton and until 1898 was called Catton Road. Traffic on the branch was never heavy, and passenger services ceased in 1930. Freight lingered on until 1950.

FIRST PASSENGER TRAIN IN PONTELAND JUNE 1ST 1905.

◁ This photograph shows the opening of the NER's Ponteland branch in June 1905. The line was built westwards from Newcastle, to serve an expanding suburban area and to connect with a much older line serving Kirkheaton colliery. There was one station on the colliery line, Darras Hall, and this was closed soon after the colliery, in the 1920s. The branch was closed in 1967, but some of the route is now part of the Tyne & Wear Metro network.

84015

THE LAST TRAIN FROM BARWICK

△ Redmire station, in North Yorkshire, seen here in a posed picture from the early 1900s, was on the old trans-Pennine line from Northallerton to Hawes Junction. Today, it is the terminus of a 22-mile line from Northallerton, serving the MOD and incorporating the reopened Wensleydale passenger railway from Leeming Bar.

Nidd Valley Light Railway.

RULES AND REGULATIONS.

I*_____ employed on the Nidd Valley Light Railway belonging to the Bradford Corporation, as_____ at_____ hereby acknowledge to have received a copy of " The Rules and Regulations for the Guidance of the Officers and Men in the service of the Bradford Corporation on the above-named Light Railway, from 12th September, 1907."

Signature,_____

Dated the_____ day of_____ 190__

* Insert full name.

To be filled up and returned to your Superior Officer.

◁ Opening in 1907 and closing in 1936, the Nidd Valley Light Railway, from Pateley Bridge to Lofthouse-in-Niddordale, was a short-lived venture. Seen here is the ex-GWR railcar it used from 1921 to 1929. Bradford Corporation operated an extension of the branch beyond Lofthouse to reservoirs at Scar House and Angram.

▷ Early in the 1960s a train bound for Whitby from Scarborough draws slowly into Hawsker station to allow the driver to receive the single-line token. Acccording to the caption on the back of the photograph, this was the last day of Hawsker as a block post.

▽ On a dull day in September 1965, a small group of boys has gathered to witness the departure of the last passenger train from Barnoldswick. Apart from the train crew, no one else seems to be lamenting the closure of the short branch from Earby, opened in 1871.

◁ In November 1982 a DMU from Huddersfield arrives at Clayton West, the terminus of a short branch off the Huddersfield-to-Sheffield main line. Opened in 1879, the branch was sustained for much of its life by local coal mines. These kept it open through the Beeching era, but the declining coal traffic brought it to an end in 1983. Today, the 15in gauge Kirklees Light Railway runs along the route.

OFFICIAL CARDS

The picture postcard was established as a popular form of communication from about 1903, and from the start its advertising potential was fully realized. Railway companies, always keen on promotion and publicity, began to issue sets of postcards, often printed in colour, to encourage traffic on their routes. The major producer of these Official Cards, as they came to be known, was the LNWR, whose catalogue ran to thousands, but others were also prolific, including the GWR. The success of these cards encouraged other companies to issue their own versions, and even some quite minor railways joined in the postcard business.

TRAIN EN ROUTE.

▶ There never was a Joint South Western and Brighton Railway. However, two famous and sometimes competitive companies, the LSWR and the LB&SCR, did work together to develop a tramway along Ryde pier, on the Isle of Wight. It opened in 1880 using horse-power and from 1887 was operated by electricity. This little joint railway, the Ryde Pier & Tramway Company, remained independent until 1924, when it passed to the Southern Railway.

▼ The Romney, Hythe & Dymchurch Railway, though a relatively late arrival in postcard terms, issued a series of Official Cards around the time of its completion in the late 1920s. Printed in colour and produced for the company by F Moore, a noted railway card publisher, these used the famous slogan 'The smallest public railway in the world'.

Joint South Western and Brighton Railway.

The Pier, Ryde, Isle of Wight.

PICTURE POSTCARD C9 LTP 6. DRAPER'S GARDENS, LONDON,

Isle of Wight Railway.

SHANKLIN.
3¼ hours from London by express trains.

PICTURE POSTCARD C9 LTP 6. DRAPER'S GARDENS, L

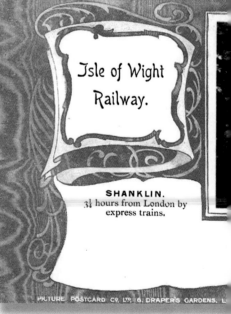

▲ The Isle of Wight's railway network was created by a number of independent companies, some of which issued cards. One was the Isle of Wight Railway, whose line from Ryde to Ventnor opened in 1866. The company remained independent until 1923.

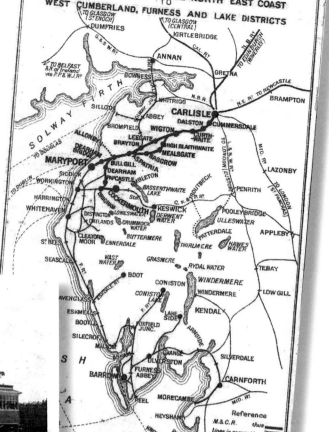

One of the most short-lived of British railway companies was the Bideford, Westward Ho! & Appledore. Opened throughout in 1908, it was closed by 1917. Despite this short life, it found time to issue a series of Official Cards. This is a classic example.

Map cards showing routes and networks were popular with many companies, including large enterprises such as the Midland. The Maryport & Carlisle was a small but fiercely independent company whose history went back to the 1840s.

Bideford, Westward Ho! and Appledore Railway.

THE WESTON AND CLEVEDON LIGHT RAILWAY.

The Weston-super-Mare, Clevedon & Portishead Railway opened in 1897 as far as Clevedon, becoming a Light Railway in 1899. It was sold in 1904 and extended to Portishead in 1907 perhaps the date of this card, despite the name variation. Later, it became part of Colonel Stephens' empire. It closed in 1940.

SHANKLIN CHINE.

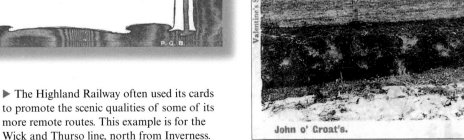

John o' Croat's.   *Wick Station*

The Highland Railway often used its cards to promote the scenic qualities of some of its more remote routes. This example is for the Wick and Thurso line, north from Inverness.

207

THE ROSEDALE MINES RAILWAY

ONE OF ENGLAND'S MOST REMOTE and spectacular railways was opened in the late 1850s to serve ironstone mines near Rosedale Abbey on the North York Moors. Running south from Battersby, the route included an inclined plane and several branches to adjacent mines. The railway was operated by the NER, and in 1864 it carried 300,000 tons of calcined ironstone from Rosedale. For much of the route the railway was at 1,000ft or more, and it crossed the watershed of Westerdale. Heavily engineered, this dramatic line closed in the 1880s, was reopened and then closed finally in June 1929. Today, the trackbed across the moors is a magnificent footpath, with exciting reminders of its industrial past.

◁ This commemorative card featuring photographs of the Rosedale mines and kilns was posted in 1972 by someone staying in one of the former miner's cottages.

▷ At Blakey Junction the branch serving the East Mines left the main line, as seen here from the only overbridge on the railway, which carries the road from Hutton-le-Hole to Castleton.

▽ Here the view from the East Mines branch across Rosedale to the well-defined main line, with its row of ruined calcining kilns, shows the quality, and toughness, of the landscape of the railway – and what a magnificent walk it makes.

◁ △ The railway's most famous feature was the Ingleby inclined plane, a dramatic piece of engineering, seen left in 1927. It was cabled-worked from an engine house at the top and carried the line up to 1,370ft. The photograph above shows the view from the top of the precipitous 1,340-yard climb. Its gradient ranged from 1 in 11 to 1 in 5 at the top, something that walkers today can certainly appreciate.

HEAVY INDUSTRY

THROUGH THE PIONEERING EARLY decades of the 19th century, the railways of northern England were inextricably linked to the development of the region's mining and heavy industry. This set a pattern that has been maintained virtually to the present day, albeit with freight traffic long since being overshadowed by passenger carrying. During the Victorian era and well into the 20th century everything that mattered was carried by train, and every mine, quarry, factory and industrial complex had its own rail network, or at least a rail connection. Today, much has gone, except for bulk cargoes still carried in dedicated vehicles, notably for mineral traffic and for the petro-chemical industry.

◁ The Hodbarrow mine near Millom, in Cumbria, was developed from the 1860s and for the next century was a major source of iron ore and high-quality haematite. The mine had an extensive railway network. Here, in about 1900, workers pose with the crew of locomotive No. 7, a Neilson of 1897.

▽ Industrial steam lived on in the North well into the 1960s. In this evocative photograph an ancient Class Q6 locomotive, No. 63458, struggles up the steep 1 in 51 Beamish Bank with a coal train.

BEAMISH

◁ Two canals, the Bridgewater and, much more important, the Manchester Ship made Manchester a major centre of industry. Much revolved around Trafford Park. Here, some time in the 1930s, a Barclay 0-4-0 locomotive owned by the flour company Brown & Polson hauls a mixed freight along one of the city's many roadside lines.

△ Among the many specialist makers of industrial locomotives, the Hunslet name was always high on the list. This brochure marks the Leeds company's take-over of two rivals, Kerr Stuart and Avonside.

△ One of the many rich mining areas of the Northeast was around Seaton Delaval. This shows locomotive No. 2 of the Seaton Delaval colliery in about 1890. Supplied new in 1855, it was scrapped in 1908.

▽ In the 1950s scenes like this were commonplace in the chemical industry. The location is unknown, but it must have been a substantial plant to have at least 31 locomotives in its fleet.

△ Many industrial companies operated passenger services for their employees. This is the 'soapworks special', run by the CWS Soap Company at Irlam, in Lancashire. A Peckett industrial locomotive of 1951 hauls an old Midland Railway six-wheeler carriage as a mainline express hurries past in the background.

◁ Many quarries had their own narrow gauge network to haul stone on site and to mainline sidings. At Hulands quarry in the 1930s, a petrol-engined Simplex locomotive, probably ex-military, pushes loaded wagons towards the crusher.

▽ Among the quarries still rail-connected is Swinden, which keeps open much of the former Grassington branch in Yorkshire. In June 1968, very near the end of British Rail steam, a BR Standard loco takes its loaded train away from the quarry.

▷ In the 1960s British Railways produced a series of stylish brochures promoting railway docks and their industrial connections. This is for Hull, and at that time traffic included grain, wool, timber, fruit, fish, coal, steel, chemicals and cars.

Port of Hull

British Railways Services to the Export & Import Trade

British Transport Docks

▷ A typical colliery scene, in this case at Ince Moss, near Wigan. The locomotive, the colliery's No. 1, was built by Robert Stephenson & Company.

No 1

MADE BY
THE DARLINGTON
FORGE L?

△ Even oversize loads travelled by train on specialist wagons, with bridge clearances checked in advance. This LNER publicity photograph shows components for the new Cunarder *Queen Mary* being transported from the foundry to Clydeside.

▷ During the 1930s all the processes of steel manufacture were railway-dependent. This shows the pouring of molten steel at the massive Dorman Long plant in Middlesbrough.

PORTS & HARBOURS OF NORTHERN ENGLAND

IN TERMS OF SCALE AND DIVERSITY, nothing could rival the dock complexes of northern England. Many had histories stretching back to Roman times, while others were entirely the creations of the railway age. Significant were those served by the east coast rivers, the Humber, the Wear and the Tyne, but there was also plenty of history on the west coast, from Liverpool up to Workington. In addition, canals and river improvements turned many inland towns and cities into ports, Manchester being the prime example.

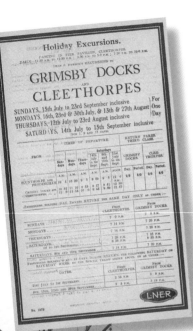

◁ This 1928 LNER handbill, promoting excursions to Grimsby docks, on the Humber, shows that visits to industrial sites have long been popular. In this case, there was also time to relax at nearby Cleethorpes.

▽ The export of coal was a major British industry until well into the 20th century. This photograph of Goole docks, also on the Humber, indicates the scale of this trade in the 1930s. Most of the coal came from the Denaby and Cadeby collieries, near Doncaster, a huge mining complex dating from the 1860s.

▽ The dock complex at Preston was developed from the 1890s, thanks to improvements to the river Ribble. Cotton and wood pulp were major cargoes and, as this 1900 label suggests, the L&YR was a major operator.

Lancashire and Yorkshire Railway.
M 56   Date
PRESTON DOCK
From
To
Via
Owner and No. of Wagon
Owner and No. of Sheet
Owner and No. of Under Sheet
Consignee

◁ According to the caption on this 1930s cigarette card from a series devoted to modern railway scenes, a traffic policeman controlled trains leaving Grimsby docks and crossing the main road! At that time fish trains left the docks every day, so he must have been busy.

POINT DUTY

G. W. R.
NEWPORT
TO
Tyne Docks
Via Banbury & G. C. Rly.

◁ Preston docks pioneered roll on-roll off services in 1948, but closed in the late 1970s. Here, in the 1960s, a dock-shunting locomotive transfers sheeted wagons to the main line.

▷ The Manchester Ship Canal, opened in 1894, turned the city into one of Britain's busiest ports, with its own extensive railway network. The phrase 'more haste, less speed' might explain this bizarre mishap to locomotive No. 29 in the 1930s.

◁ The development of Fleetwood docks started in 1877, with the active support of the L&YR, whose great grain elevator is shown here. Fishing was also important here, with over 170 trawlers operating from the port at its peak.

FLEETWOOD GRAIN ELEVATOR
LANCASHIRE & YORKSHIRE RAILWAY COY   1882

WYSE DOCK & GRAIN ELEVATOR
FLEETWOOD

BRITISH RAILWAYS
O. 6074 (B)
194
From WASHINGTON
SHIPPING TRAFFIC
To MIDDLESBROUGH
DOCK
North Eastern Region   N.E. Section
VIA
Owner and
No. of Wagon   3   Sheets In or
on Wagon
Consignee
Ship
1005/9 4,000 11/48.   W.L. 106

MINIATURE RAILWAYS : NORTHERN ENGLAND

THE HOLIDAY RESORTS of the North of England have long been famous for their miniature railways, and some of the oldest, and best known, lines are in this region. The earliest were built before World War I, at Blackpool and Southport, with Blackpool boasting the first seaside miniature railway in Britain. Others followed in the 1920s and 1930s, notably the North Bay Railway at Scarborough. In all, there were more than 20 miniature railways in the costal resorts of Northwest and Northeast England.

▷ The Sunny Vale Pleasure Gardens at Hipperholme were opened in 1880 by Joseph Bunce. There were boating lakes and, much later, a miniature railway, seen here in 1950.

▽ Cleethorpes' first line opened in 1948. In 1954 battery-powered locomotives were introduced, and in 1972 the line was rebuilt to a 14.5in gauge and extended along the seashore. In 2002 the railway acquired, and has given a new lease of life to, Sutton Coldfield Miniature Railway.

△ Skegness has enjoyed several miniature lines. The first, shown on this card, opened in 1922 with its main motive power a Bassett-Lowke 'Little Giant' locomotive. This closed in 1928. The next line opened in 1948 but had a brief life, and the third opened in 1951, a 10.25in gauge line that was completely rebuilt and reopened in 1971.

▷ A 15in gauge line, the Lakeside Railway, opened at Southport in 1911. In 1913 it was taken over by CV Llewelyn, and this card dates from that era. The line was extended in the 1940s.

▽ Blackpool's South Shore Railway opened in 1905. It was well engineered and highly popular, and the staff wore smart uniforms, as this card of about 1906 shows. When it closed some five years later, its Bassett-Lowke 'Little Giant' locomotive moved to Halifax.

▽ Opened in 1948, Saltburn's 15in gauge line ran through Valley Gardens. This card shows the streamlined diesel-electric locomotive 'Prince Charles', which was built in 1954.

The Miniature Railway, South Shore, Blackpool. Train leaving Station.   A. N. Co.

▷ One of the most famous and largest seaside miniature railways opened in Scarborough in 1931. Unusually, the North Bay Railway's route is linear, rather than conventionally circular.

THE "SCARBOROUGH FLIER" ARRIVING AT PEASHOLM STATION.

◁ The miniature railway at the National Railway Museum in York has always been a favourite with visitors. This picture shows the original 7.25in gauge line.

THE RAVENGLASS & ESKDALE RAILWAY

THE RAVENGLASS & ESKDALE is one of Britain's best-known miniature railways, yet it started life as something rather different. In 1875 a 3ft gauge mineral line was opened to serve haematite quarries near Boot, and passenger services started the next year. This closed in 1908 and was then reopened in 1915 by Bassett-Lowke as a passenger and tourist railway – though still with some quarry traffic – to promote the viability of the 15in gauge. Since 1960 it has been owned and operated with great success by a preservation society.

STANLEY GHYLL HOTEL & ESKDALE EXPRESS

△ When this card was sent in 1905, the original railway was near the end of its life. Tourism was still being encouraged, and the message is: 'We came up on this train on Friday, it was lively!'

◁ This locomotive, 'River Esk', was designed for the railway by Henry Greenly and built in 1923. Four years later, it was rebuilt as shown here, with tender driving wheels for extra power.

△ When the railway was reopened by Bassett-Lowke, it started with a variety of old locomotives. This is 'Ella', built in 1881 by Sir Arthur Heywood. It was acquired in about 1918 and scrapped in 1926.

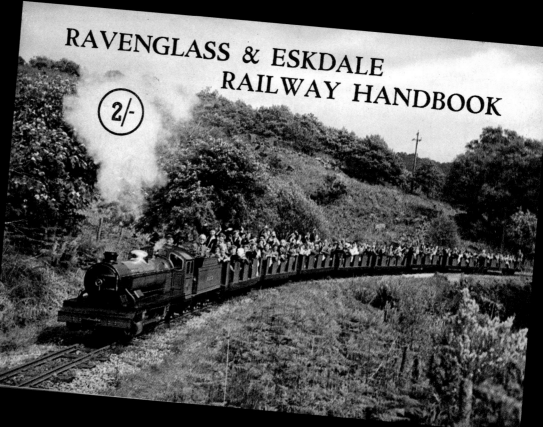

△ This card shows a later view of 'River Esk', ready to depart with a crowded train in the early 1960s. By now one of the mainstays of the railway, the locomotive was always popular.

RAVENGLASS & ESKDALE RAILWAY HANDBOOK

2/-

◁ Few small boys can resist the lure of a steam locomotive. This one seems a bit overawed by the responsibility of the driving seat.

△ The R&E has always issued a good range of publications and souvenirs. This handbook dates from 1962, soon after preservation.

TRAINSPOTTING

RAILWAY ENTHUSIASM IS AS OLD as the railways themselves, and train-watching has always had a particular appeal. Generations of children, young and old, have stood at the ends of platforms writing down the numbers of passing trains, and even today, in an age of largely unremarkable trains, the habit is alive and well. Locomotives have always carried numbers, and sometimes names, but this process was rationalized in the 20th century, making possible the publication of lists and spotters' guides. Also perennially popular are national and local railway clubs and societies, whose journals have played a vital role in the documentation of railway history, but more memorable for many are the special tours.

▲ A classic group of railway enthusiasts pose at Gloucester Central station in May 1956, in front of the locomotive that is about to take them on a South Wales tour organized by the Gloucestershire Railway Society. Just one woman is present.

▲ Trainspotting is today almost a term of ridicule, but in the 1950s and 1960s this was a universal pastime, particularly among young boys. There were various spotters' guides, including this 1960 example given away with *The Wizard* comic. The dramatic cover shows the prototype Deltic diesel overshadowing the age of steam.

◀ In 1937 a group of lucky young enthusiasts have a chance to talk to the driver of A4 Pacific 'Silver Fox', whose streamlined curves were then the latest thing on the LNER.

45402–45540			
45402	45427	45452	45476
45403	45428	45453	45477
45404	45429	45454	45478
45405	45430	45455	45480
45406	45431	45456	45481
45407	45432	45457	45482
45408	45433	45458	45483
45409	45434	45459	45484
45410	45435	45460	45485
45411	45436	45461	45486
45412	45437	45462	45487
45413	45438	45463	45488
45414	45439	45464	45489
45415	45440	45465	45490
45416	45441	45466	45491
45417	45442	45467	45492
45418	45443	45468	45493
45419	45444	45469	45494
45420	45445	45470	45495
45421	45446	45471	45496
45422	45447	45472	45497
45423	45448	45473	45498
45424	45449	45474	45499
45425	45450	45475	
45426	45451		Total 842

45500*Patriot
45501*St. Dunstan's
45502 Royal Naval Division
45503 The Royal Leicestershire Regiment
45504 Royal Signals
45505 The Royal Army Ordnance Corps
45506 The Royal Pioneer Corps
45507 Royal Tank Corps
45508
45509 The Derbyshire Yeomanry
45510
45511 Isle of Man
45512†Bunsen
45513
45514†Holyhead
45515 Caernarvon
45516 The Bedfordshire and Hertfordshire Regiment
45517
45518 Bradshaw
45519 Lady Godiva
45520 Llandudno
45521†Rhyl
45522†Prestatyn
45523†Bangor
45524 Blackpool
45525†Colwyn Bay
45526†Morecambe and Heysham
45527†Southport
45528†
45529†Stephenson
45530†Sir Frank Ree
45531†Sir Frederick Harrison
45532†Illustrious
45533 Lord Rathmore
45534†E. Tootal Broadhurst
45535†Sir Herbert Walker, K.C.B.
45536†Private W. Wood, V.C.
45537 Private E. Sykes, V.C.
45538 Giggleswick
45539 E. C. Trench
45540†Sir Robert Turnbull

"Patriot" Class
4-6-0   **6P & 7P**

*6P introduced 1930. Fowler 3-cyl. rebuild of L.N.W. 'Claughton' Class (introduced 1912), retaining original wheels and other details.
Remainder introduced 1933. New locos. to Fowler design (45502–41) were officially considered as rebuilds).
7P introduced 1946. Ivatt rebuild of Fowler locos. with large taper boiler new cylinders and double chimney.

Weight: Loco. { 80 cons 15 cwt. { 82 cons 3 cwt.†
Pressure: { 200 lb. Su. { 250 lb. Su.†
Cyls.: { (3) 18" × 26" { (3) 17" × 26"†
Dr. Wheels: 6' 9"
T.E.: { 26,520 lb. { 29,570 lb.†
Walschaerts Valve Gear.   P.V.

30

◀ Ian Allan is a famous name in transport publishing and best known of all is their long-running 'ABC' series of British Railways locomotives, trains and other rolling stock, used by generations of enthusiasts to record spotting successes. This list of LMS Patriots is from a 1955 edition.

◀ Trainspotting can be a lonely activity. Here, in the wilds of North Wales, an enthusiast, his camera round his neck, watches a passing Snowdon Mountain Railway train.

◀ Caught from a carriage window, a solitary enthusiast has crossed the dereliction of this northern scene to watch a passing special.

◀ There were many railway clubs, but the best known of those aimed at younger enthusiasts was the Ian Allan Locospotters Club. The famous Club badge was recognized nationwide.

◀ This scene would have been familiar at any major station anywhere in Britain in the 1950s and 1960s as groups of boys spent days together noting the passing trains in their spotters' books. Today, health and safety concerns would make it impossible.

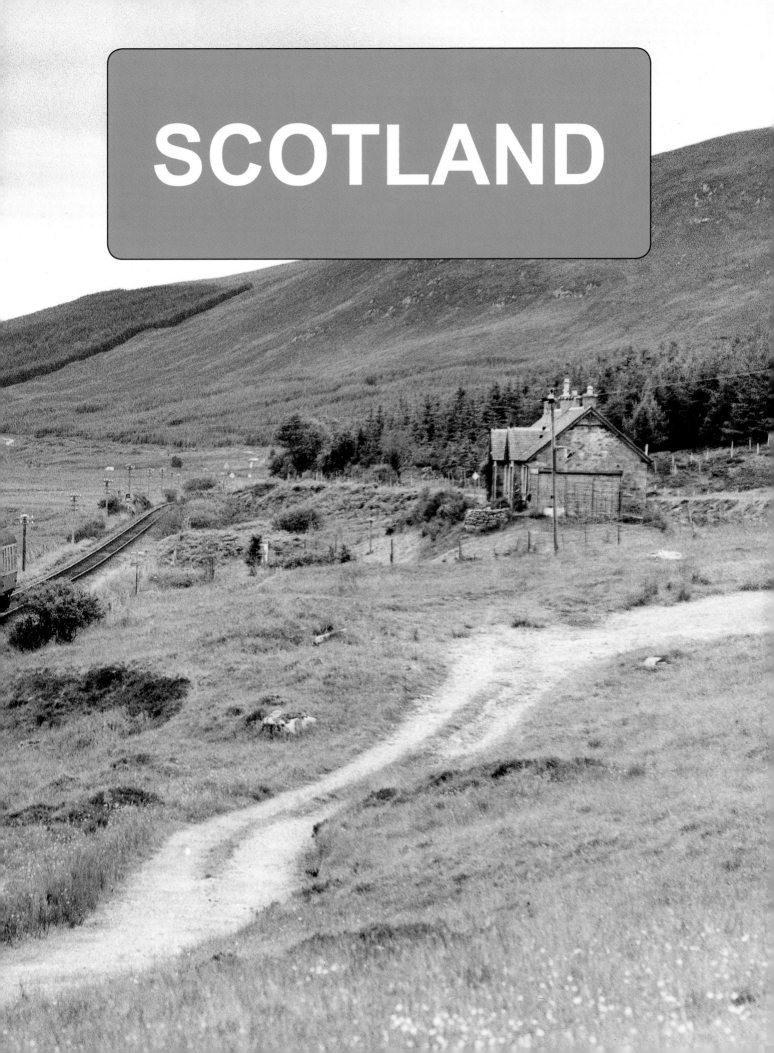

SCOTLAND

INVERNESS TO WICK & THURSO

THE JOURNEY TO WICK AND THURSO is one of the best in Britain, notable for the great diversity of landscape through which it passes. Despite the challenges posed by the terrain and the lack of population and industry in the region, the decision to drive a railway north from Inverness came early. Work started in 1862 and progressed slowly. One section was built and operated by the Duke of Sutherland, who was a major supporter of the railway. Finally, it was completed in 1874 to both Wick and Thurso by the Sutherland & Caithness Railway. Ten years later, the Highland Railway took control. The line gave a boost to the local economy, and many industries benefited, including fishing, forestry, whisky distilling and engineering. During World War I the line was a vital supply route to Scapa Flow. Since then, closure has often been considered, but the line has survived.

◁ In the 1950s British Railways went to great lengths to encourage off-peak leisure travel on many Scottish lines. As this 1956 handbill indicates, that included routes in the Inverness area.

▽ In the 1990s modern DMU units replaced the traditional locomotive-hauled trains on the route. Here, an Inverness-bound Sprinter in one of British Rail's late liveries makes its way through the characteristically magnificent and empty landscape near Lairg.

Station Square, Inverness.

△ The starting point for the journey is Inverness station, set in a square with the hotel adjacent. Built between 1855 and 1862 by the Inverness & Nairn Railway, it had a simple but decorative stone façade, shown in this Edwardian view. This was replaced by dull brickwork in 1968, but the interior is still full of interest.

△ By the 1990s locomotive-hauled trains had generally gone, replaced by the ubiquitous modern DMU. This is Invergordon, formerly an important naval base but latterly given a new lease of life by North Sea oil, as the anchored rigs suggest.

◁ This card of Invergordon from the harbour was posted in 1912. Dick, writing to his girl in Devon says: 'You talk about coming on a motor tour to Scotland. I think you had better hire an aeroplane and fly up.'

△ This Edwardian card shows a view of Invergordon from the station. It has not changed much over the years. A Highland Railway train is ready to set off towards Inverness. The black-and-white photograph at the top of this page was taken from the footbridge.

▷ The Highland Railway, like so many other companies, issued sets of Official Cards for promotional purposes in the early 1900s. This one illustrates Tain station.

225

▷ Wick and Thurso stations were built in 1874 to the same plan, with a simple train shed. Both survive largely unchanged. Here, in 1957, a Class 3MT tank, No. 40150, is ready to take the Thurso carriages to Georgemas Junction, where they will be joined to the Wick section of the train.

◁ The most eccentric station on the route is timber-framed Dunrobin, built to serve the Duke of Sutherland's nearby castle in 1902. As owner and builder of part of the line, the Duke had his own locomotive and carriage, the latter housed in the shed visible beyond the platform. Now restored, the station is no longer private.

△ The history of the line is marked by changing fortunes and changing patterns of freight. Many kinds of traffic have come and gone. The most recent arrival has been containers, many being used to supply local supermarkets. The depot is at Georgemas.

▷ A highlight of the journey from Inverness used to be the arrival at Georgemas Junction, where the Wick and Thurso sections were separated. This involved complicated locomotive movements, about to take place here in 1987. Modern DMUs have made this unnecessary.

◁ In the summer of 1951 an
ancient, dirty and anonymous
0-6-0 hauls three box wagons
out of the goods yard at Thurso
towards Georgemas Junction.
Thurso's train shed can just
be seen in the distance.

▽ In the late 1980s, a Class 37
diesel, the standard locomotive
on the line at that time, waits
to depart from Wick.

THE LYBSTER BRANCH

THE BUILDING OF MINOR RAILWAYS serving local communities was greatly encouraged by the Light Railways Act of 1894, which simplified construction and operating regulations. A typical example was the Wick & Lybster Light Railway, whose construction was funded by local subscriptions, the Highland Railway and a Treasury grant of £25,000. Opened in 1903, it was operated by the Highland Railway until it was absorbed by the LMS in 1923. The railway's 13-mile route ran south from Wick down the east coast of northern Scotland, serving small communities such as Thrumster, Ulbster, Mid Clyth and Occumster. It was never busy – in 1909 there were three trains a day each way – but local fish traffic helped. The last trains ran, largely unlamented, on 1 April 1944, but the route can easily be explored.

NEWSPAPER LABEL
1D. LABEL
Wick and Lybster Railway.
No. 2236
Carried at Owner's risk, and to be called for by Consignee at the Station to which it is addressed.

△ The line's stations were simple but functional and elegant timber structures. Remarkably, one survives, at Thrumster right by the main road, and this has been restored and given a platform and a length of track.

▽ A typically quiet summer's day at the Lybster terminus in the 1930s. A carriage waits, door open, just in case any passengers turn up. In the distance are the engine shed and water tower. On the right a line of cattle wagons represents the freight traffic that kept it alive.

▽ It is over 60 years since the line's closure, and sheep graze where trains once ran. Today, much remains to be seen in the landscape, often visible from adjacent roads.

▷ When this card was sent in 1960, the branch was a distant memory. By now, the region was attracting its share of tourists and, had the railway survived, it might have enjoyed a new lease of life.

GREETINGS FROM

WICK

BRIDGE STREET

THE RIVER

THE HARBOUR

CASTLE OF MEY

OLD MAN   A.7510

▽ The line was cheaply built, and there are few engineering features on the 13-mile route. Here, near Thrumster, a shallow cutting was carved through the gentle landscape, marked by surviving railway fencing. At some point after closure in 1944, this old horse-drawn harrow has been abandoned on the trackbed, adding another layer to the story of outmoded technology.

▷ In some places the trackbed is so intact that it seems closure was only a few years, rather than decades, ago. The route is not an official footpath, but much is easily accessible.

The Highland Railway Series   Fishing Boats going out, Wick.   Wick and Lybster Light Railway

△ The Highland Railway issued a series of Official Cards in the Edwardian era to promote traffic and encourage tourism. This one, showing the Wick fishing fleet, was specifically designed to promote the Wick & Lybster Light Railway, which the Highland operated.

THE BLAIRGOWRIE BRANCH

COUPAR ANGUS FEATURED EARLY in Scotland's railway history, and the first line reached the town in the 1830s. By the 1840s it was firmly in the network of the Scottish Midland Junction Railway, and it was this company that opened a short branch to Blairgowrie in August 1855. The town's linen mills were part of the branch's justification, but later the major freight traffic was soft fruit for jam making, particularly raspberries and strawberries. By 1866 the branch was under the control of the Caledonian Railway, becoming in turn part of the LNER and British Railways. Passenger services ceased in 1955.

▷ The Blairgowrie branch was just under 5 miles long, and the journey took about ten minutes. The intermediate station was at Rosemount. Here, in the 1950s, a vintage Class 3P Caledonian locomotive, No. 54465, storms towards the level crossing with the A923 near Rosemount with an enthusiasts' special.

▽ It is a quiet day at Coupar Angus, probably in the 1930s, with no passengers and no trade for the bookstall. The station sign says 'Change here for Blairgowrie', and the branchline train waits in the bay platform. The branch ran parallel to the main line for a while, before swinging away to the north.

London Midland and Scottish Railway Company
(CALEDONIAN SECTION).
($\frac{46}{856}$)

BLAIRGOWRIE
FROM
DUNBLANE

◁ The line's main engineering feature was the bridge over the Isla. The bridge has gone, but the iron piers that supported it still stride across the river.

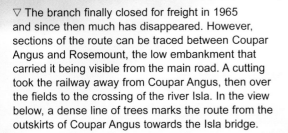

The Beech Hedge, Blairgowrie, Perthshire.
PLANTED 1745.   LENGTH ¼ MILE.   HEIGHT 98 FEET
B.26.

▽ The branch finally closed for freight in 1965 and since then much has disappeared. However, sections of the route can be traced between Coupar Angus and Rosemount, the low embankment that carried it being visible from the main road. A cutting took the railway away from Coupar Angus, then over the fields to the crossing of the river Isla. In the view below, a dense line of trees marks the route from the outskirts of Coupar Angus towards the Isla bridge.

▷ One of Blairgowrie's claims to fame is the magnificent beech hedge that runs, 100ft high, for a quarter of a mile beside the main road. It was planted in 1745 and looks as impressive now as in this 1930s card – though modern traffic makes taking photographs rather more hazardous today.

SCRAPBOOK : SCOTLAND

DESPITE THE CHALLENGING nature of much of the landscape and the relatively small population, Scotland had a magnificent railway network that reached into the distant corners of the country. The main lines that linked the major towns and cities were built first, but other increasingly minor routes soon followed. Outstanding were the Scottish branch lines, wonderful in their diversity. In the 1960s much of this network was torn apart, leaving large areas of the country with no railway at all. Freight, always important, kept some of the lines alive for a while, but ultimate closure was inevitable. Luckily, some spectacular routes escaped the axe; for the rest there are only photographs and memories.

▷ Langholm was at the end of a 7-mile branch from Riddings Junction, on the Waverley route north from Carlisle. Opened in 1864, the branch was famous for there being no trains on the Sabbath after 1865. In 1963 Class 4MT No. 43011 waits to depart. Closure came in 1965.

▽ The long Alford branch northwest of Aberdeen, which opened in 1859, had closed to passengers in 1950, but freight traffic carried on until the 1960s – as shown in this image of dog and diesel in communication.

△ Built by the North British Railway initially for agricultural traffic, the Haddington branch near Edinburgh had a long life as a freight line, although passenger carrying stopped in 1949. This is the small terminus station at Haddington.

▷ The short Penicuik branch, opened by the independent Penicuik Railway in 1872, was soon swallowed by the North British Railway. Staff pose on a sunny day in the Edwardian era. Passenger services ceased in 1951 but, as so often, freight survived until the late 1960s.

△ An early closure in the 1940s was the long branch line from Dumfries to Moniaive, yet in 1963 the timbered station building was still standing in an overgrown wasteland.

▽ The Alloa Railway completed this swing bridge across the river Forth in 1885. The steam-powered machinery used to operate it was housed in the raised cabin. Two days before the line closed on 29 January 1968, a special final swinging of the central span took place.

▽ In 1965, a year before closure, an old Class J37, No. 64608, hauls a pick-up freight train away from the fishing port of Gourdon, near Inverbervie, Aberdeenshire, on the branch from Montrose.

▷ When this photograph of Carmyllie, terminus of a branch from Elliot Junction, just west of Arbroath, was taken in 1960 there had been no scheduled passenger trains since 1949. Freight continued until 1965.

▽ In the 1980s the yards at Fort William were still busy with freight and maintenance traffic, and were home to a variety of diesel locomotives. The snow-covered hills make a suitably wintry backdrop.

▷ One of Scotland's most remote branches was the line from Spean Bridge to Fort Augustus, seen here. Opened in 1903 and operated by various companies, the branch was always short of money and traffic. Passenger services ceased in 1933, freight in 1947.

25 Pads of 200 lvs. 10-44. T.S. 9266

L.N.E. & L.M.S. RAILWAYS
(DUNDEE & ARBROATH JOINT RAILWAY)

Ⓐ
4263

4023

CLOAKROOM

DATE.............................19......

ONE BICYCLE
OR PERAMBULATOR
7d.

Declaration of Value if exceeding £5, viz. ....

Extra payment thereon 1d. per £ per day

The articles in respect of which this ticket is issued are received by the Company subject to the conditions printed below and on the back hereof, AND SUBJECT TO PAYMENT OF THE CHARGES PUBLISHED AT THE CLOAK ROOM.

The charge made on deposit covers storage for the day of deposit and next day ; for each subsequent day an additional charge will be made. The Company shall not be liable for loss, misdelivery or detention of, or damage to any articles or property which, separately or in the aggregate exceed the value of £5, unless at the time of deposit the true value and nature thereof shall have been declared by the Depositor and 1d. per £ sterling of the declared value paid for each day or part of a day in addition to the ordinary Cloak Room charges and such loss, misdelivery, detention, or damage shall be proved to have been occasioned by the negligence of the Company's servants,   (OVER

4023

ONE BICYCLE OR PERAMBULATOR

RAILWAY STATION, FORT AUGUSTUS.

37 412

THE RAIL JOURNEY BETWEEN
FORT WILLIAM AND MALLAIG

Travel by
THE STREAMLINED
OBSERVATION CAR
on the romantic West Highland
Line—Britain's Scenic Railway
SEASON 1959

MONDAYS TO SATURDAYS, 1st to 13th JUNE and 14th to 26th SEPTEMBER

				p.m.
				5 42
FORT WILLIAM	leave	MALLAIG	leave	
	a.m. 10 24	FORT WILLIAM	arrive	7 24
MALLAIG	arrive	noon 12 0		

MONDAYS TO SATURDAYS, 15th JUNE to 12th SEPTEMBER

	SO	SX			p.m.
	a.m.	a.m.			6 10
FORT WILLIAM	leave 9 20	9 50	MALLAIG	leave	7 51
MALLAIG	arrive 11 3	11 24	FORT WILLIAM	arrive	

SO—Saturdays only.   SX—Saturdays excepted.

The Observation Car, which is fitted with large windows and comfortable armchairs, will be attached to the rear of the trains shown.

SUPPLEMENTARY CHARGE FOR THE SINGLE JOURNEY IN EITHER DIRECTION

2/6

Accommodation can be reserved in advance at Fort William and Mallaig Stations.

A CONDUCTOR WILL TRAVEL IN THE CAR AND DESCRIBE THE POINTS OF INTEREST EN ROUTE

BRITISH RAILWAYS

Be sure to visit the
SCOTTISH INDUSTRIES EXHIBITION
Kelvin Hall, Glasgow :: 3rd to 19th September, 1959

◁ The long extension of the West Highland route from Glasgow finally reached Mallaig in 1901. Initially, fish and freight kept the line busy, but soon passenger-carrying became important, with an increasing emphasis on tourism. The best way to enjoy the line's scenic quality used to be from the famous observation car, advertised by this British Railways handbill of 1959.

▽ Several observation cars were used on Highland lines in the 1950s, including a former Pullman vehicle that had run previously as part of the Devon Belle. Here, in September 1958, the observation car used on the Coronation Scot in the late 1930s is turned at Fort William in preparation for the return journey to Glasgow.

◁ In February 1989 floods washed away the Ness bridge, north of Inverness, cutting off the lines to Kyle of Lochalsh and to Wick and Thurso. This is the view looking north towards Dingwall in the immediate aftermath of the disaster, with the arches of the 1864 viaduct collapsed in the river. A new concrete and steel replacement was quickly erected.

▷ The line to Kyle of Lochalsh took years to build. Dingwall & Skye Railway began it in 1868, reaching Strome Ferry in 1870, seen here in about 1890. This was to remain the terminus until 1897, when the line finally reached Kyle.

Railway Station and the Caulagh, Kyle of Lochalsh   Kyle of Lochalsh Station

◁ Kyle of Lochalsh has always been a remarkable station. Blasted from solid rock and built out over the sea, it is dominated by the view of Skye. Apart from the trains, little has changed since this card was issued in about 1910.

THE BALMENACH DISTILLERY

CROMDALE LIES AT THE HEART of a region famous in the 18th century for the production of illicit whisky. This was regularized by an Act of Parliament in 1823, and the following year James McGregor opened a distillery at Balmenach. In 1897 this was purchased by Glenlivet. By then, the Strathspey Railway's Speyside line from Boat of Garten to Craigellachie had long been open, and a short but steeply graded branch was built off it from Cromdale to serve the distillery. Closed in 1941, the distillery reopened in 1947 and was much expanded. The branch line brought in grain, coal and other supplies and took out the finished product. It was an important part of the local scene until 1969, when the Speyside line was finally closed, taking the Balmenach branch with it. Until that point, the distillery's two tank locomotives had worked the line on Tuesdays and Thursdays, with shunting in between.

◁ A card from a Balmenach shareholder, posted in 1905.

▽ The entire route of the 1.5-mile branch from Cromdale to Balmenach is clearly visible in the landscape and makes a pleasant walk. Here, at the end of a steep climb from the main line, it approaches the distillery, with the bonded warehouses on the right.

POST CARD
THE ADDRESS TO BE WRITTEN ON THIS SIDE.

The Secretary,
Balmenach-Glenlivet Distillery Ltd
Balmenach
Cromdale
NB.

◁ Shortly before closure of the branch in November 1969, one of the distillery's two Andrew Barclay 0-4-0 tank locomotives hauls loaded wagons up the steeply graded track from the goods yard at Cromdale.

▽ No. 2020, built in Kilmarnock in 1936, takes a rest while whisky casks are unloaded into the bonded warehouse. This locomotive, now called 'Balmenach', is preserved at the nearby Strathspey Railway.

▽ ▷ The branch ended at the distillery's goods yard, now immaculately grassed. The bonded warehouses are on the left, and the structure in the centre is the remains of the loading platform, seen in use in the photograph on the right.

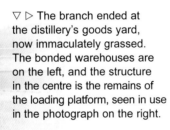

COAL TRAFFIC

THE HISTORY OF COAL MINING in Scotland goes back at least to the Roman era, and by the early 18th century Scotland's mines supplied 16 per cent of Britain's coal. Mines were established in many parts of the country, but the main producing regions were the Central Lowlands, the Lothians and Fife. In the 1950s there were more than 200 mines, and 100,000 workers were employed in the production of Scotland's Black Diamonds. This was soon to change, and within 50 years the Scottish coal industry had become a part of history. However, in the 1960s, when most of these photographs were taken, the industry was still thriving, and numerous steam locomotives were at work on the extensive network of lines and sidings serving the collieries. In many areas, this traffic was maintained into the 1990s, by which time the destruction of the industry was under way.

△ By the 1960s mine closures, along with their railway networks, were occurring in many parts of Scotland, encouraging the running of specials by various railway societies. Typical is this visitor to Annbank, near Ayr, which had lost its passenger services in the 1950s. The enthusiasts travelled in brake vans.

▷ Wagon labels and loading way bills for former collieries in Scotland are still widely available, providing an insight into the scale of the coal traffic over a long period. This NBR example dates from 1893.

△ Much of the network around Annbank survived until the 1990s, serving still-active Ayrshire collieries such as Killoch. Here, in May 1991, two Class 37 diesels haul a heavy coal train from Killoch through Annbank Junction.

▽ On a misty summer morning in 1965 an elderly Class J36 locomotive, No. 65282, makes hard work of its train of empty coal wagons from Bathgate to Riddoch Hill colliery, in the Lothian region.

▽ In 1965 Scottish steam was on the way out, but there were still some stirring sights – particularly on the coal lines. Here, in August of that year, a 'Crab', a Class 6P5F, No. 42800, makes a good show of its train of empty coal wagons for Killoch colliery, near Drongan on the line from Ayr.

▷ In another atmospheric Ayrshire view from the last summer of Scottish steam, 'Crab' No. 42909 runs tender-first at the head of its heavily laden coal train as it passes Patna on the Waterside-to-Ayr route.

Hartley COAL
From The FIFE COAL Co., Ltd.,
Bowhill Collieries, Cardenden.

To Hugh MacDonald

STATION.

PERTH & DUNKELD

Via

Wagon No. _____ Date 14 JAN 1928 Weight _____ T. C.

▽ An old J36 lets off steam as its driver has a shouted conversation with the signalman at Lower Bathgate box, in the course of shunting operations with empty coal wagons in August 1965.

SCOTTISH PORTS & HARBOURS

THE VARIED AND OFTEN CHALLENGING coastline of Scotland has long been lined with ports and harbours, many of which were railway-connected from an early date. Indeed, many lines in Scotland were built to follow the coasts and to serve the communities clustered along them. Fishing harbours great and small were one of the mainstays of the network, but also important were mineral cargoes, chiefly coal. Large dock complexes served the major cities of Edinburgh, Glasgow, Dundee and Aberdeen, with railways here and elsewhere operating as general carriers as well as serving the needs of engineering, ship-building and the military. Many ferry ports, for example Stranraer, owed their success to the railways.

▽ The transportation of coal from the mining areas of east and west Scotland to the docks was a vital activity from the 1850s to the 1990s. Here, in the 1980s, two Class 37 locomotives are backed onto a long rake of empty coal wagons that had just delivered their cargoes to Ayr harbour.

△ In this 1950s photograph an old 0-4-0 saddle tank locomotive shunts wagons among the warehouses at Leith docks. Parked against the warehouse is one of the famous Mechanical Horse tractor units, so vital in the successful operation of railway depots of that era.

△ In Aberdeen, as in many other harbour towns and cities, the quays were centrally placed and until the 1960s scenes like this were common. Here, in 1956, a tank locomotive, living out its retirement in dock use, makes it way among the cars and lorries.

△ In Aberdeen a dock shunter hauls flat wagons towards a cargo vessel waiting to be unloaded, probably in the 1940s.

△ This 1942 LNER publicity photograph shows a recently unloaded American 2-8-0 heavy freight locomotive, sent to help the war effort, on the quayside at 'a Scottish Port'.

BRITISH RAILWAYS

From WASHINGTON .... SPL ....19......

O 6074 (B)

SHIPPING TRAFFIC

To GLASGOW

Scottish Region   N.B. Section

Via BERWICK

Owner and
No. of Wagon

3

Sheets in or
on Wagon

Consignee

SHIP

1005/9 10,000 8/49

IT IS NO SURPRISE that Scotland's rugged landscape, scattered population and limited number of coastal resorts restricted the building of miniature and narrow gauge lines. Well under 20 miniature lines are recorded, though the list includes such familiar names as Kerr's of Arbroath. Even rarer are narrow gauge railways. One of the earliest briefly served the Ardkinglas estate in Argyll, and another obscure one was the Sannox Railway, a mineral line on the Isle of Arran. Tourist lines, other than those shown here, include the Rothesay & Ettrick Bay Tramway, operating from 1879 to 1935, and the Mull & West Highland, a recent arrival opened in 1976.

△ In 1938 the Scottish Empire Exhibition was held in Glasgow, inspired by the Wembley Exhibition of 1924 and designed to encourage the revival of Scotland's economy after the difficult years of the 1930s. The many attractions included a large-scale miniature railway.

△ Carnoustie miniature railway was a short line that operated along the beach between 1937 and 1939. Known as 'the Brighton of the North', Carnoustie, in Angus, was famous for its pierrot and theatre shows.

△ Kerr's Miniature Railway was opened at Arbroath, in Angus, in 1935. This substantial line has been rebuilt and enlarged several times. Part of its route is beside the mainline railway, so there are many versions of this photograph from different periods. This is the 1960s.

◁ Craigtoun Park in St Andrews, Fife, has seen two miniature railways. The first closed in the 1970s following vandalism and was replaced by a new line around the lake. This card shows the earlier, smaller-scale line.

OFF TO FAIRYLAND, CRAIGTOUN PARK, ST. ANDREWS

◁ The first railway across the Kintyre peninsula was a mineral line opened in the 1870s to serve local coal mines. As this traffic was seasonal, it was decided to expand the line to cater for tourists in the summer. Thus was born the Campbeltown & Machrihanish Light Railway, opened in 1906. It was a grand and well-built railway, with smart carriages. The route started on the quayside at Campbeltown, where the trains met the Glasgow steamers. Successful at first, it suffered from the collapse of the coal trade and closed in 1932.

▷ Scotland's most famous narrow gauge line is the Glasgow Subway, opened in 1896. Initially cable-operated, it switched to electric traction in 1935. Apart from its small scale, with its 4ft gauge, the railway was known for its distinctive red cars, which continued in service until 1977, when the network was fully modernized.

Farewell to Glasgow's Victorian Underground
1896   1977
New Underground opens 1978-1979

▷ △ The Glasgow Subway cars were, until 1977, a wonderful and much-loved legacy from the Victorian era. When the decision was made to modernize the line, special commemorative tickets were issued (above). The new subway opened in 1980 and continues to serve the city in a memorable way. It is popularly known as the 'Clockwork Orange', because of its bright livery.

CIGARETTE CARDS

THE PICTORIAL CIGARETTE CARD dates back to the 1890s, its popularity linked to the mechanization of cigarette manufacture. Cards were issued in huge quantities and with an astonishing range of subjects by a large number of manufacturers. Transport-related subjects were always popular, though aircraft and ships seemed more common than railway series. WD & HO Wills, a name particularly associated with a great diversity of cigarette card subjects, issued several railway series.

► There were many famous Wills brand names, but the most familiar was 'Wild Woodbine', with its distinctive packet design. Each pack contained one card.

▼ 'Our King and Queen' was a well-known Wills card series issued in 1937, with 50 cards to the set. In this case, the railway connection is incidental: one card shows the King (then Duke of York) in 1925 driving a miniature locomotive at a fair at Dudley.

EXPRESS LOCOMOTIVE "SILVER JUBILEE,"
London, Midland & Scottish Rly.

The interest of this 4-6-0 three-cylinder express passenger engine, completed in May, 1935, centres in the beautiful finish. The shiny black of the boiler, cab and tender sides is contrasted with the chromium plating adopted for wheels and motion work, steam pipe casings, etc. No. 5552 bears the name "Silver Jubilee" in honour of His late Majesty King George V's Silver Jubilee. She was exhibited at Euston, together with the former L.N.W.R. 4-4-0 engine "Coronation" (built 1911), during Silver Jubilee Week, May, 1935. On Nov. 6th, 1935, she worked the honeymoon special conveying the Duke and Duchess of Gloucester from St. Pancras to Kettering. (No. 1)

"PACIFIC" EXPRESS LOCO. "PRINCESS MARGARET ROSE," *L.M.S.R.*

For hauling the most important Anglo-Scottish expresses over the West Coast route, including the "Royal Scot," "Midday Scot" and "Night Scot," the L.M.S.R. employs 4-6-2 locomotives of the "Princess Royal" class, each named after a member of the Royal Family, and weighing with tender, in working order, 158 tons 12 cwt. Like the G.W.R. "King" and "Castle" class engines, these engines have four cylinders and a boiler pressure of 250 lb. per sq. in. On such duties as the "Royal Scot" express, these engines may work right through between Euston and Glasgow (401¼ miles), or Euston and Edinburgh (399¾ miles). (No. 2)

TURBINE-DRIVEN LOCOMOTIVE,
London, Midland & Scottish Rly.

The familiar exhaust beat of the orthodox steam locomotive is strangely absent when this engine is running, for the drive is by turbine and gearing instead of by cylinders and pistons. The smooth turning effort imparted to the driving wheels by a turbine and the very gentle exhaust, thus saving much basic long attracted locomotive engineers. Our illustration shows No. 6202, a 4-6-2, which was introduced in 1935, the first of the type to be built by a railway company in Great Britain. The main turbine, used for forward running, develops 2,000 h.p. and is carried under the casing near the front; a smaller turbine for backward running is on the opposite side. (No. 3)

▲ The first 'Railway Engines' set was issued in 1924, with subsequent engine and locomotive sets following in 1930 and 1936. Each contained 50 cards and, as seen here, albums were available. Further sets were issued for Eire and New Zealand.

PLAYING POLO FOR LORDS v. COMMONS.

ING POLO FOR LORDS v. COMMONS. The King, Duke of York, was a keen polo player. In the picture before the start of a match at Ranelagh Club, when he presented the House of Lords against the House of Commons in a match for the Harrington Challenge Cup. His Majesty's interest in sport, particularly in tennis, polo and golf, has been marked since boyhood. Like his father, King George V, he is also a fine shot. Swimming attracted him too and, as is the case with the Queen, he is a dancer whose skill and enthusiasm are well matched. (No. 19)

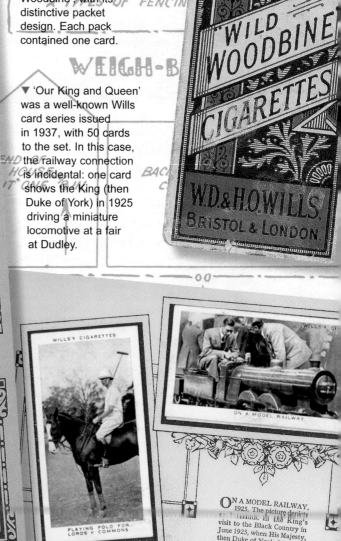

ON A MODEL RAILWAY, 1925. The picture depicts visit to the Black Country in June 1925, when His Majesty, then Duke of York, inspected a model railway at an old English fair held at Dudley. Since his Cambridge days the King has been keenly interested in mechanical science, and after the War, when radio was developing rapidly, he had a workshop of his own, in which he assembled new sets. He has driven trains, trams, motor-cycles, and, of course, motor-cars. In 1927, when on his visit to New Zealand, he drove an electric locomotive through the longest tunnel in the Dominion. (No. 20)

"DEAD MAN'S HANDLE"

LOCOMOTIVE HEAD CODES

WHISTLE

896 100

TRACK SIGNALS

GUARD SLIPPING A COACH

MOBILE CRANE HANDLING CONTAINER TRAFFIC

TRANSFERRING MAILS FROM SHIP'S TENDER TO TRAIN

▲ ▶ ▼ The most interesting Wills railway series was the 'Railway Equipment' set, issued in 1938. The 50 cards offered an insight into many aspects of the railway industry at that time, as indicated by the selection shown here. In collecting terms, none of the Wills railway series is considered to be a rarity.

VEHICLE USED FOR TUNNEL INSPECTION

GANGER'S MOTOR TROLLEY

WEED-KILLING TRAIN

251

INDEX

AUTHOR'S ACKNOWLEDGEMENTS

Photographs used in this book have come from many sources. Some have been supplied by photographers or picture libraries, while others have been bought on the open market. In the latter case, whenever possible photographers or libraries have been acknowledged. However, many such images inevitably remain anonymous, despite attempts at identifying or tracing their origin. If photographs or images have been used without due credit or acknowledgement, through no fault of our own, apologies are offered. If you believe this is the case, please let us know, as we would like to give full credit in any future edition.

For special help in tracking down rare or unusual images, for being generous with items from their own collections and for help in many other ways, I am grateful to Charles Allenby, Peter Cove, Janet & Godfrey Croughton, David Dawes, Nick Dodson, Charles Duller, John Green, Tony Harden, Brian Janes and the Colonel Stephens Railway Museum, Eddie Johnson, Alan Langham, Jean Lucas, Catherine Ryan, Anne Scott, Andrew Swift.

All Change! is the fifth book in a series that started some time ago with *Branch Line Britain*. Although broadly similar in approach, each book has represented a different challenge, and this one is no exception. The now well-established process of assembling the visual material, carrying out research, seeking out and photographing lost railways and writing the text is time-consuming, laborious, generally enjoyable, frequently frustrating and occasionally exciting. However, it could not be achieved without the support and enthusiasm constantly offered by the production team, Sue Gordon, Julian Holland, Dawn Terrey, Heather McCarry and, last but not least, Mic Cady at AA Publishing. As the series rolls on, my debt to my wife Chrissie increases year by year. I am amazed by, and ever grateful for, her patience and her tolerance as railway matters continue to fill our lives.

PICTURE CREDITS

Unless otherwise specified, all archive photographs, postcards and ephemera are from the author's collection.
l = left; r = right; t = top; b = bottom; m = middle

Photographs by Paul Atterbury: 2/3; 7tr; 18b; 19b; 21b; 23t; 25b; 41ml; 46b; 47b; 48t; 49b; 53t; 54t; 54br; 65; 66tl; 66b; 69tl; 69mr; 126/127b; 128/129b; 129b; 130tl; 131tl; 131mr; 133tl; 133b; 156l; 158b; 159b; 162m; 162bl; 163tl; 166tl; 168mr; 169ml; 169b; 180tl; 180b; 190tl; 190tr; 190br; 191tr; 191b; 192tl; 192tr; 192/193b; 194mr; 195b; 197; 199tr; 199b; 209tr; 228mr; 229t; 230; 231t; 233tl; 233b; 240b; 241br

Other photographs are by:

GP Abraham: 219t
JW Armstrong: 205tr
Ben Ashworth: 5br; 92ml; 92br; 93t; 93b; 98t; 104mr; 104bl; 105tl; 106mr; 107; 111mr
Hugh Ballantyne: 19ml; 129t; 204/205t; 227t; 234mr
GA Barlow: 184br
SV Blencowe: 31bl
Peter Bowles: 37t; 37mr; 38ml
Harold Bowtell: 172tr
John M Boyes: 241tl; 241mr
Ian S Carr: 203tr
HC Casserley: 30b; 138mr
Colour-Rail: 29mr; 58t; 122t; 134b; 135b; 139t; 157tl; 189mr; 200bl; 232mr; 234b
GH Cooper: 218ml
Stanley Creer: 146tl
Derek Cross: 58b; 59t
G Daniels: 154/155
Driver Dave: 17t
JJ Davis: 80/81; 113mr
David Dawes: 79br
G Devine: 202tr
Dreweatt Neate: 153 (x5)
Charles Duller: 250–251 (x13)
Mike Esau: 13t; 18t; 139mr; 198b
Michael J Fox: 44/45
WH Foster: 202b
C Gammell: 8/9; 20b; 171br
JG Glover: 38br
John Goss: 173tl; 236bl; 243b; 244; 245tr; 245b
GPO: 62-63
John Green: 70b; 71m; 123t; 189tl; 210b; 212m

Tony Harden: 11t; 12t; 12b; 19t; 20tr; 20ml; 21tl; 23b; 24b; 25t; 27b; 29t; 29bl; 32mr; 33tl; 38bl; 39tl; 40tr; 40ml; 40b; 41tr; 41b; 46m; 47tl; 49tl; 51tl; 52ml; 52br; 55tr; 55b; 57tl; 68b; 71tr; 73mr; 74m; 74b; 76tr; 76mr; 76m; 76bl; 77tl; 77b; 83br; 84br; 87mr; 88bl; 90mr; 92mr; 93ml; 96mr; 96bl; 99tr; 99b; 101br; 109b; 111tr; 112tr; 113br; 114tr; 114ml; 114b; 115mr; 124ml; 124br; 125tl; 126t; 130b; 131br; 135tr; 140tl; 143t; 143m; 143br; 144/145t; 144mr; 144b; 145mr; 145ml; 145br; 147t; 148tr; 148b; 149t; 149ml; 149br; 150tr; 150b; 151mbr; 151br; 157tr; 158t; 160m; 160bl; 160/161b; 161tr; 162t; 164tl; 164/165b; 165t; 165br; 166bl; 166/167t; 167br; 168b; 169tl; 171mr; 172ml; 172br; 174t; 174bl; 177ml; 178tr; 179mr; 181m; 181mr; 181b; 182tr; 182ml; 182b; 183t; 183ml; 183bl; 188mr; 188b; 189br; 194b; 195ml; 196ml; 196bl; 198tl; 198mr; 200mr; 201tl; 203ml; 203br; 204tl; 204ml; 206/207t; 206mr; 206/207b; 207tr; 207ml; 207br; 209br; 215bl; 216tr; 216b; 217ml; 217mr; 217br; 225ml; 225br; 226tl; 228b; 231br; 232bl; 235tl; 235m; 237tr; 239mr; 239bl; 242m; 248tr; 248ml; 248mr; 248bl; 249tl
Tom Heavyside: 10; 17b; 106b; 121t; 121m; 222/223; 226br; 238/239t; 243t
Robert Hendry: 249mr; 249b
Steven Hills: 34bl; 35tl; 35 tr; 35 ml; 35br
Julian Holland: 11b; 15b; 16t; 16b; 36mr; 86b; 87t; 88/89b; 89tl; 89tr; 90b; 91; 92t; 94/95b; 95tr; 95br; 136b; 137t; 137b; 224b
Roland Hummerstein: 71bl
Brian Janes/Colonel Stephens Railway Museum: 65tl; 66mr; 67tl; 67mr
Alan Jarvis: 111b

Eddie Johnson: 210ml; 211mr; 212br; 215mr; 246bl
Norman Jones: 211bl
Norman Jones & GK Fox: 211tl
RL Knight: 41tl
Alan Langholm: 201b
Jean Lucas: 218/219b
Michael Mensing: 14; 15t; 57ml; 57b; 83tl; 84t; 85t; 105b; 106tl; 142tl; 142mr; 142/143b; 147ml; 235tr
Milepost: 72ml; 214/215m; 246ml; 247tl
Andrew Mist: 85b
Gavin Morrison: 13b; 24t; 97t; 125t; 157b; 205bl; 225t; 226m; 227b; 236/237b; 238b; 246/247b
SC Nash: 168ml
RB Parr: 236tr
Ivo Peters Collection: 39b; 73tr; 109t; 109tr; 146b
Geo F Pitt: 102bl
C Plant: 147br
Robert Pritchard: 82b
RC Riley: 28t; 60t; 61b
JJ Roberts; 122b
Anne Scott: 28b
AS Scott: 227ml
WS Sellar: 103tl; 235b
Brian Sharpe: 36b; 37bl; 208b; 209m
P Shoesmith: 100tr
J Spencer: 98br
Andrew Swift 11ml; 32bl; 33br; 33bl; 34tl; 34mr; 64mr; 67br; 69br; 85b
Douglas Thompson: 177mr
RE Vincent: 26m; 27t
Bob Webster: 103br
G A Yeomans: 159t

CHAPTER OPENER ILLUSTRATIONS

pages 8/9: In June 1958 a GWR Class 5700 tank locomotive hauls a coal train up from Hayle Wharf in Cornwall.
pages 44/45: A Class 02 locomotive, No. 21, 'Sandown', sets off from Ryde Esplanade towards Ryde Pierhead in the summer of 1965.
pages 80/81: In coronation year, 1953, Tal-y-Llyn locomotive No. 4, 'Edward Thomas', takes water at Dolgoch.
pages 118/119: A busy scene in the late 1950s at Banbury Merton Street, the end of the branch from Verney Junction, following the arrival of the diesel railcar from Buckingham.
pages 154/155: In 1960 an assorted group of passengers struggle to board the train at platformless Worlington Golf Club Halt, on the Mildenhall branch.
pages 186/187: Their shift over, a driver and fireman go off duty at Heaton Mersey shed in the 1960s.
pages 222/223: Near Achnasheen, in 1984, a Class 37 diesel hauls its Inverness-bound train through landscape typical of the Kyle line.